THE ROAD
TO YOUR
BEST
STUFF

by Mike Williams

**Taking
Your Career,
Business or
Cause to the next
level...**

AND BEYOND

Published by Mike Williams Solutions, on the web at www.mikewilliamssolutions.com

Cover illustration by Michael K. Shelton
Interior design by Sheltongraphics, Inc.
Printed by BCP Digital Printing, Baltimore, MD 21215

ISBN 0-9800534-0-4
TXu-358-179
Printed in the United States of America

THE ROAD
TO YOUR
BEST
STUFF

by Mike Williams

Taking
Your Career,
Business or
Cause to the next
level...

AND BEYOND

This book is dedicated to my parents,
Lula and the late Charles Williams,
for believing in me.

I am grateful to several people for their insights, criticisms and encouraging words, leading to, and during, the work on this book. I asked several people for feedback. Their comments, critiques and questions were invaluable.

Les Brown played a key role by expecting, and badgering, me to write and publish. My wife Rhonda provided a source of comfort during a process that can be very intense. I owe them both.

My sincerest thanks to a host of friends, family members and colleagues for reading my manuscript. They are: Sue Burkhart, Karen Preston, Anika Chandler, Demia Kandi, Kristin Curtis, Lynda Jones, Andi Williams, Carole Clodfelder, Yasmin Green, Kimani Clodfelder, Joe Gray, David Hughes, Alex Whyms, and my mom. Their comments, questions, and support are much appreciated. Sue Burkhart also proved to be invaluable in proofreading this book. Her eye for details was much needed, and is equally appreciated.

In addition, I am thankful to my editor, Terry White, for his help in keeping my writing within the rules without cramping my style. Terry also helped keep me moving from one stage to the next, with a constant sense of what I was trying to do. I also appreciate the efforts of Bill Bell and Fran Frazier, who have known me for a long time, and cared enough to assure that anything I publish meets a certain standard in style and content.

The graphics, including page layout and cover design, were provided by Shelton Graphics. They understood my intent, and presented my words and ideas well. I really appreciate their work.

All in all, this book has been a major undertaking for me, and I appreciate the time and effort of every person who contributed to it.

Thanks.

TABLE OF CONTENTS

FOREWORD

When Mike Williams sent me his manuscript for review, I thought I would take a look at it, offer some comments, and send it back with my best wishes. I knew Mike and his work, so I expected it to be good. What I didn't expect was to get swept up by it. After all, I read self-help books on career and business issues all the time.

Almost immediately, I found myself writing notes in the margins, underlining points, and pausing to work through the issues and questions that were being raised. I started out working on the manuscript, and ended up working on myself. Mike has been my mentor for over 30 years and the business strategist who helped me start and grow my business from zero to my first million-dollar year. So, I should not have been surprised that his first book would be something of value, something worth reading, working through, and passing along to others.

I first met Mike Williams in 1970 at a community event where he was speaking. I liked his perspective and told him I thought he would make a great addition to the radio station where I was program director. Mike was a respected activist, but I saw him as a strategic thinker and communicator.

Several months later, there was an opening in the station's news department at the same time the training program where Mike worked was ending. He contacted me, and I convinced the general manager he was right for the news job. Mike started at the station a couple of weeks later, and right away made his presence felt, on the air, around the station, and with the listening audience. That was 1971, and we have been working together ever since.

Right away, we began to work on bringing community issues to the airwaves, matching my energy and passion with his more measured way of looking at things. Our styles might have seemed like oil and water, but they mixed and matched in a way that has been solid and productive over the past 35 years.

Mike was the person who saw things in me as a broadcaster and communicator that I didn't yet see in myself. He helped me channel my zeal into effective community awareness and record-high voter registration campaigns. He helped me in my efforts to run for public office, win my first campaign, position myself effectively on legislative issues, and get bills passed.

In the middle '70s, I began my study in personal development, reading everything I could get my hands on. We were on similar paths. We would compare notes and explore ways to do something with what we were learning. The common goal, always: to change the world.

So, when I started 1986 with the New Year's resolution to throw my hat into the ring as a motivational speaker, I called Mike to put together a plan to help me take the field by storm.

I call Mike my mentor, but in practical terms, he was the business strategist who helped me formulate a plan to become a successful entrepreneur, a pioneer in public speaking, and someone who was making an impact on the lives of people from the classroom to the board room, and many other places. He is still the big-picture person who gives direction to my major projects and ventures.

Mike didn't just work with me. I was reminded of his "stuff" in my conversations with others about his work. Before I was able to retain him to guide my business, Mike had worked with lots of business owners, at the various levels. As reflected in this book, his expertise in marketing and management is solid, and his insights have made an impact on entrepreneurs, non-profit executives, political leaders, community advocates, authors, physicians, entertainers and others.

I truly believe that The Road to Your Best Stuff will help thousands of people with big dreams become successful. The process the book introduces will help them see their careers and themselves in ways they might not have even imagined. I began putting things to work, even as I was reading. It slowed down my feedback to Mike, but it helped me understand, and speak to this book's real value.

This book has power. Let's put it to use. ◣

—*Les Brown*

INTRODUCTION

⌁ About the Title

For our purposes in this book, your stuff is the set of qualities you possess that, when combined, form a foundation for what you can achieve or accomplish in your life. Your stuff is the essence of what you have, including your strengths, your ideas, your skills or talents, your experience, your habits, your standards, and your passion, as applied to your life's work, whatever the work might be. It is the fuel for what you can do or accomplish.

World-class achievers in various fields start with varying levels of skill, drive, confidence and expectations. In aiming for your best stuff, we are looking to maximize opportunities for you to achieve at your highest level, even if it is not at the highest level of your special gifts or strengths. In the same way that it works for the highest achievers, it works for others. With the right mindset and the right skill set, all kinds of things can happen, to bring your best stuff to the fore. How you get there is: The Road To Your Best Stuff.

⌁ About the Book

This book offers a new perspective on achievement. It is based on my 25 years of work as a consultant and trainer, and a longer period of preparation through a series of jobs, projects and experiences. It is also based on interviews and observations, formal and informal, with people who were at various stages of reaching for and attaining success in a variety of fields. It includes experiences with established and startup business owners, heads of grass roots and large-scale nonprofit organizations, public agencies and public officials, and a wide array of civic, community and business leaders. It draws on my experience as an activist, a broadcaster, a trainer, a program manager, a program analyst, and many other job experiences whose greatest combined value was to allow me to see a larger picture of achievement and to appreciate the challenges, pitfalls and breakthroughs that occurred along the way.

What these people have in common is a desire, or at least a wish, to distinguish themselves in their respective fields and in many cases to reach some measure of financial success in the process.

Having worked directly with scores of consulting clients on hundreds of projects, having trained several hundred others, and having interviewed and observed even more, I have seen patterns of accomplishment, outright failure, and a reluctance to reach fully for obvious potential. Each of these patterns deserves our attention. The pages that follow provide some of that attention, with an emphasis on the requirements for establishing a high level of success, and continuing that success to higher and higher levels.

This book also reflects my work with a number of consulting clients. Many of them will be nameless for our purposes. The most notable exception is my long-standing role as a career and business strategist for motivational speaker Les Brown. Our collaborative work, presenting programs and products in the field of personal and professional development, ties into my own work as a marketing and management consultant for Brown and several other high achievers. In fact, the work with Les, and the many people I have met and observed through that work have influenced my perspective, directly and indirectly, and the advice I offer to clients on a much wider scale.

So, we will connect large-scale, continuous success to the mastery of four dimensions--personal, professional, organizational and promotional. Whatever your field of choice, the pages that follow establish an approach for rising to the next level, and the one beyond that. Often, the examples given greatest attention involve unconventional careers, many of which seem to be growing in popularity. Simply stated, it is necessary to be strongly connected with the attributes that are fundamental to who you are, in order to establish a foundation for long-range and continuously rising success. As important as it is to master the skill set that can make success achievable and repeatable, it is the mindset that will determine the extent of that success via the habits it takes to repeat success.

Beyond paying attention to the personal dimension, your personal side, your impact will be connected to getting to know the professional requirements for success in your field and where *you* stand in the midst of things. The challenge in the professional dimension is to develop a process for assuring that your level of mastery meets the standards for your field, and, beyond that, becomes the basis for your ability to distinguish yourself among your peers and in the circles where your credibility and viability are determined.

Once you are clear about who you are, what you've got, what you want, and where you are, in terms of your personal and professional development, you can effectively address the necessary, but often overlooked, organizational dimension, and its role in helping you rise from one level to the next. To go far beyond where you are now, you have to identify, attract and incorporate key people, and the resources they bring, into your effort. Virtually nothing of major consequence happens between a great idea and a great and repeatable achievement without the involvement of others. So, attention must be given to organization and a keen awareness of how your work habits might help or hinder your ability to maximize resources and build a career, business or cause that can sustain itself and continue to grow.

When you have a sense of yourself as viewed in personal, professional and organizational ways, you can effectively focus attention on the promotional area, where you create the connection between your stuff and the requirements of the market-place. Unlike the professional dimension, where you look at the technical and informational aspects of a field, in the promotional dimension you are developing strategies and efforts for approaching and actually succeeding in the marketplace. Aside from how good you are at what you do, or the quality of what you offer, it is important to have an awareness of yourself from the vantage point of those who hire, support or do business with people who do what you do.

By exploring several fields, and learning from people whose lives and careers provide obvious examples, we are better able to determine a course for ourselves and a handle for our future. If you have no aspiration for changing the world, your life or your field in some dramatic way, then what follows may have little meaning or value. On the other hand, if your aims are high and your intentions are serious, this book can help you do something special with your stuff.

We will explore in the coming pages how your view of yourself will determine how hard you work, how good you become, the quality of resources you attract, and how well you are able to gain, repeat, and elevate success. The resources we attract go a long way in determining how far we go and how much we can achieve. How we see ourselves will play a major role in determining the quality of relationships we form, the extent to which we can build trust, the ease with which we present ourselves and our stuff in the marketplace, and how well other views are considered and factored into our decisions.

When I was midway through writing this book, I ran into an old buddy whose track record in business has earned the envy of many who know his accomplishments. He has earned millions through a variety of ventures, having lots of reasons to feel good about what he has done. But in our conversation that evening he made it clear that he sees himself as an underachiever, someone who didn't get further because he was not comfortable in his own skin. He said he didn't feel that good about himself and it stopped him. His candor shocked me. We hadn't talked in depth in a number of years, and it seemed that those years had taught him some things about himself that he didn't mind sharing.

No doubt, when you have a limited view of yourself and your possibilities, it blocks your commitment to good habits, promotes poor decision-making, and lowers your expectations. And once expectations are lowered, everything negative falls into place to assure that your grasp stops far short of your reach.

There is no question that what you know can make a big difference in how far your business, career or cause can go. But as successes begin to mount, and you are looking for ways to go to higher and higher levels, more of the keys to breakthroughs will come from your inner search. The better you know and accept yourself, the better prepared you will be for the challenges at the higher levels. ◣

1. Preparation

1

CHAPTER ONE:

The Personal Dimension

TO reach some major goal or milestone of achievement and sustain it, you will need a solid sense of who you are: your own history, your ideas and aspirations, your strengths and weaknesses, the values and standards you hold, and other things which make you *you*. Who you have been is a key to who you might become or what you might need to overcome, to establish your special place on the planet.

1. Examine who you are, what you want in your life, and why.

Actively explore and get to know yourself in the most practical ways, below the surface and beyond the obvious.

Step back and take a long, hard look at yourself. If you take the time, it can be revealing. Consider your strengths, weaknesses, loves and hates, ideas and experiences--the collection of things that define you. This self-examination process is very important for determining what is likely to be satisfying for you, personally and professionally beyond your immediate time and place. Before even considering where or how you want things to go in your future, take some time and effort to get a fresh sense of who you are uniquely and fundamentally, and who you have been in your past. Get help from those you trust to get a solid assessment.

Where have you been? Part of what distinguishes you from others is your personal history. When you examine the events, the people, the lessons, the joys, the hardships, the aspirations, the breakthroughs you have experienced, you see something that is uniquely yours, uniquely you. Just knowing what matters and how it serves to structure your real priorities helps you know how you might organize and live your life more meaningfully.

In addition to the role your personal history plays in help-ing to distinguish or define you, your aspirations say a lot about who you are. In fact, your aspirations help to shape your decisions, which help to account for your history to date. You are shaped by what has happened to you, by what you allowed to happen, and by decisions and priorities you chose that made things happen. You owe it to yourself to pay attention to all of these things. Those who jump into careers without a solid sense of who they are, and what fits for them, can end up on a path that makes no sense for them, in a career that does not feed them internally.

When you think about what you want, consider the things you would value as keys to your legacy or your purpose, things that would make all your efforts worthwhile. And depending upon where you are in your life, the question raised, and how seriously it is likely to be taken, is at issue. Teenagers pursuing careers in the performing arts, sports, broadcasting, modeling or architecture might have little interest in asking the why question. They are more likely to care more about how. As one who pursued engineering based on identified skills and the reported salary scale in the late '50s and early '60s, I made a decision to ignore the profiles that suggested that writing and other creative areas would probably be more fitting and fulfill-ing. It did not take long for my career to crash, beginning a long journey to meaningful work.

Before you start to put together the resources to move your career or business dramatically forward, be clear about where the appeal lies, what part of your stuff is being addressed or expressed. The why sets the stage for how. Entrepreneurs who know why they want to be in business, and not just to make money and be independent, save themselves loads of stress by digging a little deeper and exploring the questions surrounding the kind of business that suits their expertise, their goals, their values, their needs, and their passions. When you make the investment in time, energy and money, you need to have a sense of the payoff in non-monetary, as well as monetary terms. So, the things you get to know up-front can shape the approach you take in pursuing your path, to best express your unique stuff.

Money can be a strong motivator in the earlier stages, but going to higher and higher levels usually requires more than a financial incentive, unless the goal itself is money. Money is usually only part of the goal, a measure of success or a means to other successes. And if money is the only substantive goal, it complicates ways for others to stay involved and to ride out the challenges that you, and everyone else, are likely to face.

The current American preoccupation with celebrity ups and downs in popular media, when put into a less gawky and more practical framework, provides a useful way to look at ups and downs in our own lives and careers. If there is something useful in knowing about the fall of pop music idols or Hollywood stars, it is most likely the fact that the details of their lives *might* provide some insights into our own, seemingly more ordinary lives.

As I see it, there are no ordinary lives, or perhaps there are no extraordinary ones. Each one is unique. Each one matters to those involved. A failed marriage, a return to drug rehab, or a battle with eating disorders is a private and ugly detail of someone's life, whether experienced by actors, singers, plumbers, fashion designers or truck drivers. If the details of celebrities' lives can be understood in ways that give insights into the lives of non-celebrities going through similar stresses, then the collective gawking might have some value beyond our collective curiosity.

The recent explosion of cable and satellite television channels and programs has provided some surprising new avenues for looking at our lives and career aspirations. A cable TV show outlining over a period of several episodes the challenges of opening a new, upscale restaurant and another show following an entrepreneur's expanding hair salon business detail the hurdles each entrepreneur faces in situations involving the perils of explosive business growth. Both shows give clear indications of how personal issues play out, when critical situations and important decisions are being made. Tempers flare. Things go wrong. Poor decisions are made. Along with taking much of the mystery out of the entrepreneurial process, the shows illustrate much of the unglamorous detail, along with some of the excitement, that accompanies a thirst for owning a business and making it successful.

I am still waiting for the movie or television series that takes a look at barber college. It could be at least as interesting as the movie, "Barbershop." I would imagine the same could be said for beauty school. I know the former situation firsthand as a customer during college days, and there was plenty of colorful chatter and drama among the students and some sparks between students and dissatisfied customers, who might not like the trainee's practice cut. The show I envision might not get as much action as "The Apprentice," but it could be as raw and dynamic as cable TV's "Film School" or "Flight Attendant School" and more authentic than those shows put together via the manipulated producing that has driven "Real World," and other reality shows. And considering the number of people who plan to make a living taking care of other peoples' hair, there might just be an audience for it. It would have potential for great drama. We would see people struggling with themselves and each other as they project future livelihoods. Who they are would be examined in a way that might do someone some good. However, in the hands of a zealous producing crew it would probably end up with fistfights, bleeped-out words and would-be barbers or stylists being separated by the latest Jerry Springer wannabe. Maybe the challenge of getting real value from reality TV will require some active thinking, looking below the surface and discovering things that were incidental to a producers plot but with useful insights, intended or not.

You might not get it from watching television, but you can't get very far toward the next level in your business or your career, and sustain it, without a good assessment of yourself, who you are in the midst of things. Often dismissed or devalued in the interest of getting things rolling, a solid self-inquiry can lead to places you might not otherwise explore, providing answers to questions you might not ordinarily ask. And you would be better off by being better informed.

In garages and driveways all across the country are weekend mechanics who tinker with their cars and those of their friends. For most of them fixing engines is a way to make or save some money and pass the time doing something they enjoy. For most of them it is a hobby, even a hobby that pays a little. For some it is the beginning stage of a larger enterprise they have always dreamed of having. They have the capacity and the desire to find out what's wrong and fix it, like the "car guys" on National Public Radio. Many businesses are examples of part-time interests that became full-time ventures, because they became lucrative enough to provide such an option.

Most weekend mechanics are not on their way to full-time careers in auto repair. It is either not deemed that important or that feasible. However, if it is what you want, what keeps you up at night, you can't afford to take it lightly. Auto repair--like woodcarving, scrap booking or interior design—either hits you or it doesn't. If dabbling or tinkering is good enough for you, then clearly your part-time interest has no full-time draw. It is probably not something you are yearning to dig into and take to a higher level. Knowing what is not important can be just as important as knowing what is.

On the other hand, a cause that occupies a special place in your life could be more important than any traditional career pursuit. Putting your efforts into a political campaign or movement, plunging into a charitable or human rights organization could become the primary way in which you focus your thinking and your energies. Your cause could become your career. If so, it is important to examine yourself and the role it might play in your own life and in the larger world. If it really has meaning, are you willing to give yourself credit for trying, or do you really want to make something powerful happen? Consider the idea that if you give it your best, and you continually make your best better, you might be pursuing a course that will change the world, if only in a small way. Impact might trump income from your perspective.

2. Know your baggage, what you need to overcome.

You need to know yourself in many ways if you want your stuff to shine. So if you ask yourself the question, "Am I ready for major success?" it is important to be honest and accurate. If the question creates discomfort, it probably means you'll face obstacles in moving ahead. If the answer is given without any real thought, it probably means that the whole issue of getting to know yourself seems unnecessary. Big mistake. Many people go through life never asking themselves such questions. Others offer glib, top-of-the-head replies when asked, providing a false reading, a false positive on readiness for the bumps in the road ahead. The reality is that we all have baggage of one sort or another, some set of negative experiences that at the very least cause us some anxiety or self-doubt. And most of us know that if we are haunted by something in our past, it will find its way into our future. Be forewarned! The key word is "haunted." It is a commonly known fact that people often overcome negatives in the past to become overwhelmingly successful and make great contributions in their fields. What inspires some might kill the dreams of others.

Unfortunately, you can't push a "hold" button or "fast forward" your development process. If there is serious, unfinished business, it needs to be acknowledged and factored into the scheme of things. A failed marriage, a costly financial decision, a troubled childhood, a bad career move, an emotional job loss, or anything else to which you are emotionally attached can get in the way of efforts to *sustain* success, even if they don't prevent you from initially *achieving* it.

Because support is so important, I always ask my clients, and people I interview, about the extent and nature of their support. Several years ago in discussions with an author/speaker about taking his career to a higher level, I asked about his team, his backup. When he replied that *he* was the team, I knew there might be a problem greater than selecting the right people to fill this role or that one. I asked if there wasn't someone, a family member, long-time friend or business associate, or someone from his past he might seek out who had expressed an interest in his career.

His face showed the answer. Blank. I had seen this person command an audience, so I knew he could communicate with larger numbers of people and from a distance. I also had seen that his interaction with people away from the platform was stiff and uncomfortable. He approached me after overhearing a conversation I was having with a client. He knew he had gone about as far with his business as he could go by himself, yet he seemed unprepared to ask for or effectively use help, no matter how much he might have needed it. He would have paid for services to the extent his budget would allow, but it wouldn't allow much. He was alone and uncomfortable. He knew it. I knew it. And he knew I knew it. It was awkward trying to have a more in-depth conversation with short time and others around, so I gave him my card, and wished him well. He needed some coaching, and had he called, I would have tried to make a good referral. Maybe he got connected through someone else. I don't know. I never heard from him.

One thing to bear in mind in the process of getting a good handle on yourself is that you can't really get to know yourself without observations and input from others, especially others who care about you. So, when you examine things in your past that might hold you back, the opinions of close supporters are important. Their candid opinions and insights need to be factored into your own thinking about who you are, how you are, what you can use and what you need to discard, to go where you want to go. By the way, be certain that the people you enlist to help have a history of actually supporting you. Don't lay yourself bare to anyone, other than a professional, who hasn't already shown they care and want to see you succeed. Peers are often more comfortable seeing you right where you are, rather than moving dramatically ahead.

If you are uncomfortable trusting people, meeting new people, or managing people, for example, you will have a steeper uphill battle in getting what you need for the next level and beyond. Be mindful that others will play critical roles in various stages of your career, whatever your field, so try to load up for your journey with people who will help you to succeed over the long haul. If you have serious trouble accepting criticism or advice, you have a built-in hurdle that others, including your competitors, might not have.

Acknowledging your weaknesses, to yourself at least, is as important as touting your strengths. We all need to determine what stands between where we are right now and where we want to be ultimately. Continuous improvement in the key areas, by the way, is critical to continuous growth and sustained, large-scale success. But the *big* thing is having a level of awareness of yourself that allows you to use your strengths and expand them, as you contain and shrink your weaknesses.

Once you fully answer the overall question concerning your readiness to move, it is important to identify where you think the difficulties might be. Yet being unready or only marginally ready for success, and the habits likely to produce it, should not necessarily put you into a position of retreat. Many people succeed, not in spite of their difficulties but in some ways *because* of them. They use those difficulties to energize themselves and focus their efforts. Recognizing emotional readiness or emotional hurdles provides good information from which to reach out for resources, get help and strengthen your effort. Your past and current supporters, and those you add to the fold, will become a collective point of reference for your success over time. They provide a framework for useful feedback and continued growth for the long road. Ask for support, and embrace it for the gift that it is. It can serve you well.

3. Respect your body and its role in your future.

Whether your chosen field involves substantial physical skill or not, remain mindful of the role that physical health and fitness can play in your life in general, and in the pursuit of a major goal in particular. Often people are too unaware or too casual about making sure the body is up for the challenge. We often hear the expression that we are nothing and nowhere without our health. Plans to be successful presume, first, that you will be here and, second, that you will be physically up for the challenge.

Not many years ago my report to an organization's CEO left a bitter taste, when I called special attention to the need for a fitness regimen as part of his strategy for success. And it became part of our ongoing discussions as to his progress in handling a range of matters he needed to address to move his company forward. His business plan was ambitious, but his fitness plan was not. He had no plan to be here.

I don't know how long I will be hanging out on planet Earth, but I know that this vessel that carries me around requires major consideration, not minor or casual attention. Having lived now more than 60 years, I am conscious of the things I would like to do, and respectful of this house I am always in. Perhaps it is age, but I can remember many years ago starting to tie my physicality to my vision of myself, and the clearer that vision, the clearer my responsibility. It just made sense. Now it is so clear to me that I have a hard time remembering any other perspective.

No one doubts the importance of a sound body for aspiring athletes, soldiers, or firefighters. Yet in the same way that athletes and others need sound bodies for the work they have chosen, there is a standard of fitness that each of us faces, unique to the individual body and the individual aspiration. Big dreams need bodies that can carry them out. Physical exams, exercise programs, more health-conscious eating, and a respect for the role of rest, including sleep and relaxation, are all essential elements of a program to take your career or business to the next level, sustain it, and move beyond.

For those who want to skimp on fitness and blame a busy schedule, it might serve them to know that Secretary of State Condoleezza Rice can find time, with a much busier and more demanding schedule than virtually all of the complainers, to get her daily workout in. She makes no bones about its importance to her, and she is not carrying around a lot of excess weight to lose. She *could* be carrying around a lot of stress, though, and she has said that the gym is a good place for her to leave it.

I came to the get-fit-for-life camp later than many people, having neglected my physicality until I hit my 40s. And I did not come along peaceably. I smirked at runners and their counterparts. But that was before I turned 40 and woke up. I couldn't afford a bright red sports car to get me over the mid-life issue. I started working out before I stopped my smoking habit, but the former seemed to help me address the latter. My driven personality could easily have taken me further down the road to bad health. Luckily, it didn't. Nowadays I probably sound as zealous as a new convert to religion. My 50s and 60s have shown a progressively greater respect for my body than earlier years. As a good friend and fitness trainer used to say on her voice mail announcement: "If you don't take care of your body, where in the world are you going to live?" If you want your body to take you someplace special, give it what *it* needs, so that it can give you what *you* need.

4. Get into your spirit.

In spite of the prevailing winds in mainstream American culture, I am not convinced that you need to subscribe to an organized religion to achieve, elevate and expand your success. Many people are doing well without religion. There are also people who succeed without any real sense of spirituality. Unfortunately, if they are operating in a complete spiritual void, they are denying themselves an invaluable reservoir of insight and support in the face of wide and complex challenges, in their efforts to set, and reach a higher and higher mark for themselves.

In calling for spirituality as an important part of maximizing your stuff, I am really talking about the value of having a body of faith or principles to which you are connected, devoted and accountable in the way you live your personal and professional life. For many people this means a traditional religion, with leaders, services, places of worship, rites, writings and its own traditions to support it. For others a spiritual identity might be less structured or defined. The key is to know its meaning in your life, and to allow it to assist you in becoming a better person in all aspects of your life.

Bear in mind that when you press forward to a new and higher level of achievement, a new direction, a new cause, or a new venture, faith is too powerful a force to be taken lightly. Heed your own calling. Invest the time, energy and thought in a conscious process of connecting yourself to higher ideals as you aim for higher achievement.

5. Know where you are you going, as specifically as you can.

Moving forward hinges in part on how well you weigh your options in setting priorities and making decisions. And the destination matters. Being uncertain about direction, values, ideas and standards makes effective planning a virtual impossibility. This means you can't effectively evaluate progress and make the necessary adjustments along the way, if you don't have a clear sense of where you're headed.

What we are dealing with are the things in your thinking that declare who you are from a career, business or social impact perspective. I come across people all the time who are plugged into jobs or careers that don't reflect any substantial measure of who they are. Often the disconnect between ideal work and actual work produces a kind of going-through-the-motions mindset. Why should we expect it to be different?

Bobby knew before his teen years that he wanted to be an over-the-road truck driver. His inspiration came from the miles he logged in the passenger seat of his dad's truck as he rode some of the nation's busiest highways on an adventure that still lights his eyes when he talks about it. He and his younger brother both have the bug. Now in his 40s, he is as excited about mastering the road as any aspiring musician, ball player or architect is about achieving success. Bobby owns his own rig, tractor and trailer, and is determined to grow his company into a small fleet over the next several months. He is headed for the next level with every expectation of getting there and beyond.

Captain Mike didn't grow up with the goal of sailing for a living. Once he worked on a sailboat, though, he knew he wanted to do nothing else. When he got the chance to buy the 26-footer he had captained for someone else, he jumped at the chance. So, when he sets sail he is not just earning a living on a sailboat, he is putting his passion to work in his own enterprise, in waters he really treasures, facing a sunset he loves to share.

Very often, career and business decisions are based on the breadth of opportunity, perceived or real, in the marketplace. What is most obviously accessible, though, might not be the most appropriate choice. The wide-open door might be leading you to a success that doesn't serve your long-term need or your vision for your life. Unfortunately, many people are stuck in places where they really don't want to be, doing things they don't want to do. Sometimes we discover that what we have is a wide-open opportunity to go down the wrong path.

I recently met a woman who had had the opportunity to achieve her childhood dream. She worked her way through college with good grades and lots of promise. Then she was accepted into law school, where she distinguished herself. Not long after graduating from law school, she passed the bar in her home state and became the lawyer she had dreamed of being since her days in elementary school. Her whole family was proud. Yet after working first as a prosecutor and later in private practice, she found herself disillusioned with the field of law and searching for a new career.

Something about the notion of practicing law had a strong enough draw to keep her working through undergraduate school and working even harder through law school. But the ways of the law as she saw it practiced caused her to rethink how she wanted to make a living. Maybe she was a bit naïve about the legal system and how she might fit into it. Maybe she saw too few other options for someone with her skills and zeal. Whatever the reasons, she now makes it clear that she has lost her desire to practice law, even with its deep childhood roots. She completed the requirements for the field, but she missed the requirement that it provide a measure of personal satisfaction. That was lacking. Despite the advice of family members, friends and colleagues, she is now going in a completely different career direction, determined to do something else.

If you lack a clear idea of what you want to do with your stuff, do what is satisfying as much as you can, even if it is as a career sidelight, until you get a better picture. Sometimes your best fit will grow out of your experience in learning and doing what is most satisfying, and it can take time to get there. So, if you do what you *must* in order to afford to do what you *want*, you might discover opportunities in either situation.

When you set out to raise your level of achievement, be sure you are on a path that is genuinely yours. And the questions that ask why are just as important as the ones that ask how. Clear, serious and candid thinking about your aspirations, ideas, values and standards in your career or business is critical for developing the plan that can take you where you want to go. And you owe it to yourself to take a good, hard look, to be certain just where it is you want to go. After all, if you don't clearly define the path that is yours, you could end up walking someone else's.

6. Figure out who's going with you.

Very few accomplishments of major proportion happen without the support of trusted family members, colleagues or friends. They are the key figures in your base of support. The reality of moving through tough times is that the input of a trusted group of people can be invaluable in weighing options and priorities, making good decisions, creating key inroads, and evaluating your progress at critical stages.

Strong families are not a pure *necessity* for taking things to the next level. Too many examples of high achievement occur *in spite of* family life, rather than because of it. Yet strong, solid families and good friendships have a unique capacity to help in shaping direction, making decisions and forming other relationships. Usually long-term friends, close family members, mentors, spouses or committed partners, and other long-term supporters are honored to be asked to be a part of the team. Ask them.

Your base of support, your team of friends, advisors and other supporters, can become a valuable frame of reference for the challenges and opportunities you are sure to face. Look for three characteristics when building your base:

- **the ideas or expertise they bring to the table**
- **the contacts and other resources they have and are willing to share**
- **their ardent support of your efforts to succeed**

Entertainer Jamie Foxx, winner of the coveted Oscar for his portrayal of the late Ray Charles, makes no bones about the importance of his support team in keeping him grounded, yet moving forward. He attributes much of his success to his late grandmother's guidance, giving him a foundation from which to build a career and a winner's outlook. He also gives a nod to a close-knit group of friends and colleagues who have been with him for several years, long before his movie and television roles and his music raised his professional stock to its currently high level.

Foxx has said in television interviews that he has been helped tremendously by having people around him who hold him accountable, both for keeping the ego in check and for keeping him out of some of the potholes that often accompany high-profile Hollywood success. They also help to assure that he maintains standards and stays on course for the goals he wants to achieve, goals which to Foxx are apparently more important than the glitz and glitter that often dominate the attention of many entertainers who receive similar applause and acclaim.

One thing Jamie Foxx did not mention in the interviews, and might not even be aware of, is that not everyone can hear the kind of feedback he is willing to hear. It is perhaps an additional credit to his late grandmother that he is receptive to hearing the all-important bad news that goes along with the always-welcome good news. Foxx deserves credit for remembering the life lessons that make it easier for trusted friends and others to help him by being willing to hear the bad news along with the good.

In contrast with Jamie Foxx is the situation faced by an up-and-coming public speaker I met in a training session. Because of the novelty of his youth, at only 18 years old, David gets extra credit for his speaking skills, and it frustrates him. He aspires to be truly great as a speaker, and he gets very little feedback that could help him improve. The problem is not terribly hard to solve, but it will take recognition by his parents, insightful teachers, career advisors and others who want to see him succeed that good critiques are essential for his future success. Fortunately, David knows he needs it, raising the issue with me. That shows his level of seriousness, and bodes well for putting the important tools into place. David is talented *and* coachable, and I would bet good money that his success as a future public speaker will reflect it.

You need cheerleaders, but you also need conscientious critics. We all do. Professional colleagues can be an important resource if they show a sincere interest in your success. Experienced peers can be full of ideas and insights, but they are often full of envy as well. Some people like the *idea* of helping others, but have a bit of a problem with the *reality* of it, actually being on board when it matters. And that's okay. Just do your best to determine who will be there when they are most needed, using behavior as the best indicator.

Try to determine each person's commitment by asking directly for support. Any real reluctance should be taken as a sign to look elsewhere. And you have to make it okay for them to decline, or they will fake it, a lose-lose proposition. You need to know who is on board, and insincerity sets up potential conflict and disappointment. Once you know who is committed, let them know you appreciate their support. Later, you can get into the respective roles you would like them to play.

7. Keep everything in balance.

A number of situations we get into reward us for having a sense of balance in our lives. High-pressure, high-powered, high-profile, high-performance people, those I call the HPs, might well be headed for high stress, high blood pressure and other unwelcome highs in their efforts to multiply their success. They need to have a practical, day-to-day sense of how work, interaction, relaxation and play feed each other, and to understand how sustaining their effectiveness is helped by laughter and other aspects of good, old-fashioned fun.

High achievers too often underestimate the importance of getting off their mental treadmills, going from task to task or from project to project with no break in intensity. They need to create a vehicle or process for transitions. Disengaging, stepping back, can help prevent their lives from being dominated by the momentum of things outside of them, things that have too much power merely because we concede them without thinking.

Managers and others who take deliberate pauses between meetings do themselves a favor by creating transitional moments to move more naturally from one problem scenario to another. It affords them less likelihood of carrying the full emotion from one situation to the next. Breeeeathe as they say in the gym. If done effectively, managed transitions are a big favor to those being managed, and to the manager.

8. Be willing to do the work.

A friend who found herself trying to untie herself from emotional issues in her past was seeing a psychologist as she tried to solidify a relationship with her significant other, while living temporarily on opposite American coasts. They were in couples counseling, and she also was getting one-on-one attention. She learned something in the sessions and in sitting at home afterwards that she liked to pass along. Her statement, her mantra, is worth bearing in my mind when attempting to go further, climb higher and do better, and that statement is: You've got to do the work.

She knew that the time in therapy was important, but she came to understand that real progress occurred after she and her friend went home. It all boiled down to whether they implemented, or seriously tried to implement, what they and the therapist determined was needed.

The same holds true in other areas. Rhetoric reduces to action, and at some point the action is all that matters. All the planning and strategizing goes nowhere, if unaccompanied by a serious effort at doing the work. So, if your personal fitness trainer writes a program for you, for instance, it will typically include things to do after you leave the training session. Most people can't afford to get fit by utilizing a trainer each time they need to exercise. In most cases, trainers provide advice, techniques and support for efforts to be carried out when they are not around.

It is an unpopular but simple fact that explosive growth in your career or business requires working hard and working smart, in order to be sustained. And try not to get too enamored of the smart part. Hard, thankless, unspectacular work will be required. Truth.

Like many, I am always impressed with talented people in all sorts of fields who really *get* the work thing, just as I am disappointed with superstars who don't. People such as rookies in pro football who study film, hit the weight room hard, and really push themselves through their drills, and first-year teachers who invest time in lesson plans and subject matter, have much better chances of building successful careers than those who slide by, even those with more raw talent. The same is true for dancers, guitar players and all sorts of others who establish a solid practice and study regimen, to ensure their readiness for the times when a high-level performance is needed. Indeed, all careers that have the potential to take our skills and talents to higher and higher levels seem to have the common thread that they have no reliable shortcuts and no guarantees of success or longevity.

Our effort is something each of us can control, and it is the closest thing to a guarantee we are likely to find on the road to maximizing our stuff on the planet. It is not merely a desirable option. It is an absolute requirement. Accept it! Hey, *embrace* it!

9. Give people a reason to want to help you succeed.

As difficult as it is for some people to admit, we need others to help us reach the really high places in life. No matter how smart we are, there are limits to what we can know about the road ahead. One of the things that surprised me when working with Les Brown in the late '80s was the degree to which people wanted him to succeed. Many competitors on the speaking circuit wished him well and spoke highly of him, and people who heard him speak worked to get him into places he could not get into on his own.

If you are willing to ask for help when you need it, give thanks for the help you get, and give credit where it is due, those who believe in you will do more than you might expect. If you think of asking for help as an admission of weakness, get over it. And if you are unwilling to acknowledge an insight or a tip from someone else as a boost to your success, you are likely to have less of that success. Don't let a big ego keep you from telling the world how much good someone did, because you can't afford to be without the support that the credit is all about.

* * * * * *

When we have a passion to do something great with our stuff, it is important to be aware of what that stuff is, even if we haven't quite figured out how it fits into a career picture. It is important to know that if designing clothes or designing landscapes is your passion, even if it is not obvious how you will make it happen or how it will help you pay the bills, it should not be ignored. A career or business opportunity should not be dismissed simply because the road to success has not been identified. Many entrepreneurs, performers, inventors, activists and others have used their unique combination of skills, experience, ideas, and energies to move forward when there were no obvious paths to success.

Our stuff, your stuff, represents something connected especially to your attributes, ideas, skills, insights and experiences. If you carefully examine what that stuff is, how you propose to tap into it, and get ready for the challenges ahead, the venture will be well worth your time and effort. ◣

Answers and Actions Needed

1. Are you clear about your stuff and what you want to do with it? Make an appointment with yourself for some serious thinking and writing. Work at it! Get clear, to get going and keep moving!

   Note: If you find yourself struggling with how or where to apply what you have, invest in a career profile, available on-line and via other career resources, or find a life coach who has experience in career matching.

2. Schedule a lunch, coffee or another meeting in a comfortable setting with your key people, and declare your career intention. Ask for some candid feedback on your prospects and problems in getting to your destination. Take notes! (A life coach can help, if you are shy of supporters or people with whom you feel you can be honest.)

3. Factor the feedback from supporters into your self-inventory, and determine where you need to work most and least. How will you work on yourself? The question is not whether, but where and how you need to work on yourself, to be ready for ups and downs and for useful criticism.

4. Make a commitment. Once you are clear about what you want to do with your stuff, make a decision to acknowledge its importance and make it a priority in your day-to-day life.

5. Decide to work on yourself, mentally, physically and spiritually, to prepare yourself for achieving at the highest levels. Get the advice of knowledgeable friends and professionals to develop daily and weekly routines, and special moments to stay focused and grounded.

6. Determine what would represent the next level for you, and the level beyond that. What are the signs or measures that would indicate success by your definition?

7. Make the argument for your success. Write out the points that give you reasons to know you can succeed. Be persuasive! Make the argument so strong that it can override any negative talk, yours or anyone else's.

8. Who's going with you? Figure out the people you think you can count on, to help you move forward. Don't be judgmental! But be realistic!

9. Ask your supporters to accompany you on your journey. Don't assume they know what you want and need. Ask for help. And keep asking.

10. Use the music that moves you! Find a role for inspirational music and word passages, to soothe and move you through hard times and daily drudgery.

11. Be thankful, consciously, not only for your stuff and the opportunity to do something special with it, but for the help and the helpers. If they appreciate who you are, what you've got, and what you want to do with it, they are a blessing.

12. Dig in! Be candid and complete!

Consider these resources to add to your own:

- *Do What You Are, Discover the Perfect Career* by Paul D. Tieger & Barbara Barron-Tieger

- *Learned Optimism: How to Change Your Mind and Your Life* by Martin Seligman

- *Health and Healing, the Philosophy of Integrative Medicine* by Andrew Weil, M.D.

- *Live Your Dreams!* by Les Brown

- *The Power of Purpose, Living Well by Doing Good* by Peter S. Temes

- *You: The Owner's Manual; An Insider's Guide to the Body That Will Make You*

- *Younger and Healthier* by Michael F. Roizen, M.D. and Mehmet C. Oz, M.D.

- *Body and Soul* Magazine, **www.bodyandsolmag.com**

- *Spiritual Literacy, Reading the Sacred in Everyday Life* by Frederic and Mary Ann Brussart

- *8-Minute Meditation. Quiet Your Mind. Change Your Life.* by Victor Davich

- *What Color is Your Parachute? 2007: A Practical Manual for Job-Hunters and Career Changes* by Richard Nelson Bolles

- *Discover What You're Best At* by Linda Gale

- *Strengths Finder 2.0* by Tom Rath

- *The 9 Steps to Financial Freedom, Practical and Spiritual Steps So You Can Stop*

- *Worrying* by Suze Orman

- *Who's Afraid To Be a Millionaire? Mastering Financial and Emotional Success by* Kelvin E. Boston

- *Self* Magazine, www.self.com

- *Fitness* Magazine, www.fitnessmagazine.com

- *Psychology Today* Magazine, www.PsychologyToday.com

- *Choosing Your Future* CD Series by Les Brown, www.les-brown.com

2

CHAPTER TWO:

The Professional Dimension

1. Know your field.

Learn the requirements for getting into and succeeding in your field.

Many people who are pursuing or planning to pursue careers in fields as different as grounds keeping or bookkeeping, bodybuilding or homebuilding are all studying the avenues where the talent they have might be put to use. Having that kind of familiarity matters ultimately, but only if there is a kind of professional mastery as a foundation. There is a big difference between mastering a craft and making a living, but the common tendency to fast-forward ourselves down the path to career success is something to be avoided. The American preoccupation with instant results gets many people looking at style over substance, and practicing the end-zone dance before learning how to catch or run the ball.

Students in high-technology fields learn a lot about currently known applications in their respective disciplines, but without active antennae, keeping up with the changes, they will be stuck in the mode that was current at the time they were in the classroom. Computers and ways to use them change so much, so fast, that Information Technology grads often walk across the stage with degrees that are already obsolete.

Many fields are changing dramatically, either because of emerging technology or emerging trends in the culture or the economy. Therefore, if you are really serious about fully utilizing your skills or talents, you will need to make the commitment to keeping up with the areas where your talent or skill might be applied.

Be good at what you do. In addition to staying on top of

what is happening in your field, mastering your art or craft, beyond how well it pays, and where it might be used, is very important to the process of setting and maintaining a standard of performance that you will maintain throughout your career. Practice, experience, critical evaluation and adaptability are all keys to continuous growth in your skill or talent. In fact, there is no real substitute for being good at what you do, no matter your chosen field, no matter the obstacles. Talent speaks volumes. Mastery of skills opens doors. Talent or skill does not guarantee success, but it is probably the best place to invest, to ensure your greatest chance.

A few years ago, pro basketball star Allen Iverson got far more attention than he wanted in sports pages and on television and radio sportscasts by his comments undermining the value of practice, as compared to game time as a point of his efforts and attention. He was being criticized by his coaching staff, and his refrain, aired time and again on television, was to the effect of "Practice! Practice?! We're not talking about games. We're talking about practice." I would bet good money that high school coaches all across the country seized those comments as a way of teaching and preaching the importance of preparation and practice, precisely because of their impact on the games that follow, including immediate and subsequent games. There must have been many high school hoops players cursing A. I. for the extra laps they had to endure because of his comments.

Iverson was much younger then, and he has shown in many ways since that time that he *gets* it. His Olympic play in 2004, where he was named team captain, was clear evidence that he understood, and his former coach, Larry Brown, who had become his Olympic coach, appreciated the difference. In an era in which game highlights overshadow fundamental and less obvious keys to winning, it is easy for young athletes to focus on the obvious. And athletes are not alone in that regard. Practice creates opportunities that show up in the glamorous moments. Musicians, actors, photographers, beauticians, carpenters, ballplayers and others need an appreciation for preparation and practice as a basic element of building and sustaining success.

At some point we each need to adopt the kind of active role in our respective careers that will allow us to know the dynamics of success and what it will take to meet them. When we examine the world from the *inside-out*, as we are doing now, there is no real place for determining what we must do to be successful. We are primarily absorbed in how we would like things to be. Later in this book, when we start to look at things from the *outside-in*, we begin to factor all sorts of things into our thinking. We start to see opportunities in a context, along with the obstacles between where we are and where we want to be.

There will always be emerging, new requirements or standards for gaining entry into certain competitive careers. When it comes to barbers, massage therapists, doctors, teachers, and many other professionals, the requirements for entry into the field are regulated. In those cases, it is easier to know exactly what it takes. You complete the requirements, you meet the established standards and you pursue opportunities as they reveal and avail themselves.

When Keith worked his way out of the barbershop where he had built his clientele and into his very own shop, he took his license, his haircutting experience and many of his customers with him. He picked a location less expensive than the one he had left, but he got a lease he could afford, a complement of other barbers he had worked with, and he handled the licensing, equipment and facility requirements for the new shop. He also drew upon some experience in remodeling to paint, add electrical outlets and install chairs, sinks and mirrors. Keith did his homework, and when he opened, he was ready for business. He didn't know all he would ultimately need to know, but he had no problem making the transition from being a barber in someone else's shop to being the chief barber in his own shop. Barbering as a field is fairly straight forward, with a fairly well defined path. Establishing a solid clientele is the next step. Then, ownership is another level altogether, as every entrepreneur learns.

Before Keith was ready to open his own shop, he had to establish himself as someone who was flat-out good at what he did. I had seen customers waiting for Keith when there were other barbers available. And the other barbers had been fairly successful before their younger colleague had come onto the scene; some of them had to watch as their customers asked for the new guy. Whatever it is that makes a barber stand out, Keith has it. His next challenge will probably be in making his shop a more solid reflection of his skills, ideas and standards. Otherwise, he might very well max out as an entrepreneur, if not as a barber.

Many fields have no well-defined criteria for entry. Over the years, I have met people with membership cards in the Screen Actors Guild who would like nothing more than to be busy on a movie set, rather than just being busy, or pretending to be. The Screen Actors Guild requires proof of employment in order to join, as does the National Speakers Association. But there are far more people with membership cards than there are those making a living in many such organizations. I also know that you can go from being a future restaurant owner to a former restaurant owner in no time at all. The ease of getting into a field has no connection to being successful in it.

As different as some fields are in terms of gaining entry and achieving success, the greatest common denominator among many paths to success seems to be the extent to which talent and effort are well matched. Later in this book, we will explore other factors which combine with talent and effort to create great opportunities and great results.

Whether or not the requirements for entering your field of choice are tightly structured, you need to be aware of the requirements for getting a foot in the door. It is important to get the best reading from those in the field or those you know have good insights into it. People within your base of support, or those you might be able to add to it, can help you weigh the information you obtain from industry insiders, libraries, the Internet, professional journals and other information sources, to get a clear picture of things. You need to know the doorways into your field, and how to gain access to them, however difficult, mysterious or exclusive they might appear to be.

Obviously, entering a field is different from succeeding in it. And though it might be more difficult to determine what it takes to *succeed* rather than gain entry, the greater issue of success is something that needs to be examined.

One of the fastest growing fields in the '90s was personal training. It continues to be popular, but the standards for entry were so minimal in the early days that some of the people I knew who were highly qualified too often could not distinguish themselves from their less qualified counterparts. Gyms were overrun with pretenders, wearing the official-looking tee shirts, the ultra-confident attitudes, and usually the better-than-average physiques, which combined to make them seem more than capable. Now, many of those who know how to sculpt bodies effectively and safely are working part-time or working elsewhere, because they were unable to establish a substantial enough clientele that would allow them to get paid in accordance with their expertise.

The best aren't always the most recognized or the best paid. This is not an argument against the importance of professional development, nor is it an argument against the prospect of a successful career in personal training. This is an argument for looking at the totality of the issues surrounding your prospective career success. Especially in highly competitive areas, distinguishing yourself will require that you be aware of personal, professional, organizational and promotional issues that will need to be addressed.

When Suzanne opened her new fitness studio in the summer of 2006, she did so with greater promise for growing her business and taking advantage of her long-standing professional reputation. With more than 20 years of experience and a long string of clients, she has paid attention to her credibility by gaining and maintaining high quality certifications and standards for effectiveness and safety. Now that she has a studio large enough to incorporate classes as well as training, she will get an opportunity to test her potential to expand her client base and move to a higher level of success and impact. Among her decisions will be her process for negotiating agreements and hiring people who can see a win/win by helping her build her shop and her business.

There are organizational and promotional issues, explored in later sections, which, when properly addressed, can make a great difference in each person's success. It is enough to say here that the quality or depth of knowledge, talent or skill will not be sufficient for success, but for the long haul it certainly will be necessary.

2. Get help in determining how good you are.

Set a process of continuously evaluating and upgrading your skill or talent level.

As stated earlier, it is one thing to know what it takes to gain *access* to your field, it is another to know what it takes to be *successful*. So, when you know the rules of entry and the road to success, you need to get a handle on how good you are. No doubt, there are ball players and horn players in abundance who have been told they are good. Some of them are. Many of them are not. The difference is the standard by which quality is measured.

The road to Yankee Stadium, Broadway, Wall Street, Hollywood, the Mayo Clinic or HGTV is built on useful, well-received criticism and the insight and help it takes to put the best criticism to work.

How good are you, and how do you know? Forget the first part of the question, and focus on the second part. The real thing to know about your talent or skill is that you need people around you who can help evaluate your status and progress, so that ultimately you meet the standard that allows you to present and represent your stuff.

Talent is, of course, difficult to measure and evaluate. Not all fields have levels of attainment as clear as professional baseball, for example, where a player might start at the level of Single A, then move to Double A, and Triple A, before being called up to the major leagues. Many players peak at the Single A level. Others make it to the major leagues and to elite status within the majors. Still others get caught in the middle, never getting to the top, or getting to the majors for only a brief stay, yet they are able to call themselves professional athletes. No other American sport has the comparable levels of skill and compensation as represented in baseball, from which out-standing players with household names and huge paychecks emerge.

Not only is there no comparable example of a well-defined ladder in other American sports, there may be virtually no other profession where such a path of opportunity exists. Apprenticeships in the trades certainly lack a comparable financial upside. Most people struggle in fields where some mysterious combination of skill, drive, personality, experience and contacts provides opportunities to move into higher levels of recognition and compensation.

In completely different circumstances, I have watched aspiring public speakers honing their skills in various Toastmasters meetings who would go to great lengths to be drafted into the speaking industry with a no-cut contract, assuring them a certain minimum income, barring injury, for a certain number of years. And there must be at least a few dancers in regional companies, actors in community theatre, or newly graduating computer engineers across the country who would love to have the opportunity to be on an established track to the big time and the big bucks. Judging by the thousands of people who have stood in line for a chance to audition for "American Idol," aspiring singers might like to see a defined ladder of success for their careers, as well. It isn't going to happen, and on closer examination it might not even have the same appeal for the career wish list. It might be a track into mediocrity or a distraction from what might be ultimately more desirable or more satisfying.

A former client I worked with in the late '80s told me of some major improvements he made in his orthodontics practice, some years later, when he began reviewing his clinical techniques. Talmadge already had a successful practice, but he was eager to improve his efficiency, to reduce complications and the overall time his patients were spending in braces. By studying state-of-the-art clinical techniques taught by a nationally recognized orthodontics expert, he improved the quality of his own work and that of his assistants, and earned big points with referring dentists. He was already certified as an orthodontics specialist in his state, but Talmadge wanted to build a reputation for going beyond established standards, to set a standard of his own. His professional reputation became front and center, and his practice grew as a result.

Most of what you are able to accomplish in applying your stuff at the highest levels will be done without the benefit of a career net or a simple system to draft you through the steps from novice to superstardom. Whether you are on your way to becoming a photographer, illustrator, psychotherapist, runway model or massage therapist, the track you find yourself on might have to be the one that you actually create.

3. No matter how good you are, invest in getting better.

It is one thing to get input from others to help determine just how good you are at what you do, it is another to recognize that your talent or skill needs continuous attention and development. In fact, arrogance has cut short many a career from reaching its full potential. You need the confidence to perform, but you also need a measure of humility, to know that you can continue to get better. And if you can get better, why wouldn't you? Especially if you want to go further, you have to be committed to your craft, whatever it happens to be.

I have no doubt that my friend and colleague Les Brown will continue to get better and better as a speaker. He has the capacity to connect with audiences that others would like to have and others mistakenly think they already have. To find the heart of an audience and touch it, especially with a variety of audience types, Les finds the often elusive connecting point at which his speech can do what he wants it to do. This does not mean developing and refining a given speech. It is something larger. As a podium speaker, and as a radio broadcaster, he creates a connection, a buy-in, with individuals while speaking to the audience as a whole. He goes into a kind of mental space where people are invited to share his vulnerability and his humor, to get his insights. Les' artistry is not just in giving a great speech, but in finding the speech within the speech which audiences tune in to hear.

Les is an artist at the podium, and though I have worked with him for many years, I rarely see and hear him speak. In an event in Chicago early in 2006, I was reminded of his gift and his commitment, not only to the audience, but also to the art of the platform speech. Unlike many of his peers, he works as hard, getting ready and delivering on stage, in his 60s as he did in his 40s.

When multiple-Oscar-winning actress Meryl Streep describes her preparation for a new role, it seems pretty obvious that being conscientious and committed to the work shows up in the quality of her performance. In-depth interviews by James Lipton of Bravo's "Inside the Actors' Studio" provide a way to appreciate how artists like Streep and others work away from the spotlight, to make the most of those moments on center stage.

Over the years, I have watched some bright people, many without much formal education or training, move into areas of greater and greater responsibility as they increased their base of skills and people savvy. The rise from clerical assistant to office manager or business manager invariably includes having effective verbal and writing skills, a knowledge of record keeping and financial matters, the savvy to identify and report problem areas and potential solutions, and an ability to gain the confidence of peers and higher ups. Good office managers and good personal assistants are worth far more than can easily be accounted for on the resume or the job description. But those who establish themselves as able to handle the pressure and the deadlines that accompany the position often earn respect and compensation that surprises those who are used to a much lower salary ceiling. They get paid for being good, and the smart ones keep getting better and raising their value.

Developments in communication technology and the increase in the number of successful micro-businesses have increased the demand and the opportunities for high-performing "virtual assistants," administrative support people who can work from anywhere and serve clients they rarely if ever see. Telephone answering systems, document preparation software, computers, and the Internet allow a savvy assistant to be shared among several professionals and have their efforts multiplied by effectively adding other solid assistants, sometimes located in various places, to their ranks.

4. Get to know the emerging trends.

As you study the developments in your field, and this is critical for any area you deem important, you need to stay on top of things, to assure that you don't get caught unprepared. Change happens! Whether due to emerging technologies and the opportunities and challenges they present, or due to changes in the economy or other things outside your control, it is important to know what is new and what can be expected. Education and training are good career insurance, but there is usually some lag time between changes in the dynamics that govern your field and the incorporation of those changes into classrooms and seminars.

After spending some time in the world of radio in the early '70s, I find myself paying at least some attention to how it changes and adapts. Back in the day, everything was fast-paced, very little talking, and no space, no dead air, between syllables. FM was new and fighting for credibility. The deejays wanted their shows to be "tight." Les Brown was still talking more than the industry trends suggested but Les was such a dominant presence that the rules bent to accommodate him. In the news department I was fighting for more minutes and more resources. Nowadays news is such an afterthought that the shift would have driven me out, if I hadn't left on my own.

In an era when syndicated shows are common, I am fascinated by the local versus national presence. Tom Joyner moved from doing shows in two cities, flying every day, to going nationwide, broadcasting in cities throughout the country. His show uses an on-air staff located in different cities, sounding like they are all in one studio. He even uses pre-taped handoffs to local station personnel, to make it sound like he is there locally. And it works. His show is very successful.

By contrast the "Satellite Sisters," five real sisters from Connecticut, are breaking new radio ground with their talk show on XM Radio, the satellite company. They talk to each other and to their audience from different cities in a relaxed format, though their energy levels and interests vary from sister to sister. Their separateness, the fact that they are in different cities, is a key element in their show. And because they are all talkers they have mastered the tip of letting people know that this is Sheila or this is Monica. They have turned radio back into a vehicle of conversation, an actual show of people talking to each other. Imagine that. Like any fields, radio is changing, and in some ways for the better. If it is your field of interest, it pays to keep up.

5. Be aware of any unspoken challenges you might face.

Bigotry can be a dream stopper.

Many people, in the middle of a quick rise to prominence, find themselves running into barriers that they weren't warned about and don't make any real sense. Weight, race, gender, age, height, gender style, skin color, hair color, religion, hair style, language, clothing style, speaking style, ethnic background, physical impairment, or other peoples' take on these things, often get in the way of career opportunities that would be clearly warranted on professional grounds. It is a reality. Bigotry can make life hard. Buying into bigotry can make success impossible. And it is better to know than not to know both of those facts.

The late Earl Woods took it upon himself to assure that his son Tiger would have a keen awareness of the bumps and potholes in the road ahead in the world of golf. His lessons would probably not have been much different if his son had shown a passion for something else at the age of two. Tiger was not surprised at the intrusions that might have become distractions in his rise to prominence for someone less aware and less prepared. Now that he has become the dominant player in professional golf, and the most dreaded player to be closing in on the final round of a tournament, his skill in handling the pressure and ignoring the negatives is legend.

So, when a youngster aspires to be President, it pays to know the challenge, all forms of it. On the other hand, some of the greatest human achievements occur precisely because of the willingness of people to ignore the challenge or override it by their commitment to doing whatever success required. They didn't buy into the negative conversation about their possibilities or the barriers other people tried to place between them and their goals. It is useful to be aware of any unspoken challenges you might face, but it is critical that you don't let that awareness lessen your commitment or define your expectations. Rising to the highest levels and sustaining it often takes a combination of unwillingness to listen to or to believe the voices of doom, however well intentioned. It takes confidence and a solid sense of yourself, as discussed in Chapter One. Big dreams, even the unreasonable ones, are the domain of those who have the dreams. Ultimately, what others think of your dream is none of your business.

6. Push! Intensify and focus your energy and time on your craft.

It is one thing to want to pursue a demanding career. It is quite another to invest the unglamorous, tedious effort it takes to do something poorly until you can do it a little better. You might have to be terrible for a while. Then, the sustained effort to get better in small bites will test you. The uphill challenge will help you answer the question: Do I want this badly enough to do whatever is required?

Listening to the artistry of a concert pianist rarely takes us to the issue of what it takes to be able to play with such apparent ease. We hear the music, rather than the struggles to develop the skills to present it. Talent separates good pianists from great ones. Practice also separates those who *wish* they were good from those who really *want* to be good. You have to *work* at it. Push!

7. Be Flexible!

Be willing to adapt, to make the most of new opportunities.

Often we need to go to new places and new sources for information and opportunities. Relocating is a challenge many professionals on the rise have to face. Television and radio broadcasters know as well as anyone that where you are can have a lot to do with the range of career options you face. This is not to say that all broadcasters should have to keep a packed bag nearby or that all would-be actors ought to be heading for one of the coasts. The process of learning and developing can happen in a number of settings. Local, regional, college and vocational programs can be important in launching careers in a number of fields. Urban areas are especially rich in career preparation resources. But new thinking can be as important as new venues in boosting your business, your career or your cause.

Stay flexible, or adaptable, in order to take advantage of opportunities that might otherwise get away. Moving might be part of a well-grounded strategy. Add training or experience that would help maximize your uniqueness, even if it is not in the handbook of conventional learning paths. Be willing to do what needs to be done to move forward, whether or not it is part of the original thinking or the original plan.

8. Maintain a sense of perspective.

Balance confidence with humility, to keep you on track.

Often I am involved in workshops with aspiring public speakers, who typically see themselves as people who are changing the world. I like to ask if they believe that they are gifted. Virtually all of them, the humble and the full-of-themselves, say yes. That reply is my opportunity to talk about the contradiction between feeling gifted and showing arrogance. If you believe that through genetics, parents, teachers, mentors or the grace of God, you are able to offer your pearls of wisdom to audiences far and wide, then it must follow that you owe some debt of gratitude that might cancel out some of the arrogance that is so commonly found. The point usually gets at least some affirming nods, if nothing else. Athletes, authors, artists, agents, lawyers, CEOs, politicians and other high performers might benefit by asking themselves the same question.

The reality is that there are many opportunities for the ego to go into overdrive when we achieve a noteworthy level of success. When you have people in your base of support who have your permission to watch out for that ego, they can help you avoid unnecessary hardships that prevent success from being repeated and elevated.

Keep them close enough to whisper in your ear, when the applause gets too loud for you to resist. It is healthy to think that the expression of great talent is something that comes *through* sculptors, singers, writers, carpenters and chefs, not *from* them.

* * * *

When you respect your stuff, and know how you want to use it to make something extraordinary happen, it is important to recognize the role that professional mastery will play. You have to begin with being good, and continuously work toward becoming better and better, if you expect to be highly successful. You need people in place to help you evaluate the quality of your game, whatever you plan to play. And you need to be committed to doing what is required to get inside the door, along with a commitment to being your very best once inside the door, to give yourself the best chance for sustained success.

To execute at the high levels, you have to be prepared, personally and professionally. Preparation sets the stage for execution. ➤

Answers and Actions Needed

1. **How do you know how good you are?** Ask your group of supporters, colleagues and available professionals to assess your skill level and what you can do to improve.

2. **Ask for help.** The better your team of caring critics, the better your chances of getting useful information. If asking for help or accepting feedback is hard, handle it by working on yourself and your personal issues. A life coach can help.

3. **Use the help you get.** Supporters will continue to provide help if you make efforts to incorporate the information and advice into your work.

4. **Make the commitment to improve continuously.** Invest time and energies to match your goal. Study! And use what you learn.

5. **Develop a practice routine** that allows you to validate in your own way what you are learning and to form good habits.

6. **Stay on top of emerging trends** that might provide opportunities or render past opportunities obsolete. Professional associations are a key. Inquire, join when eligible, and participate!

7. **Be relentless with your efforts!** Be willing to be unreasonable, matching your passion to rise with efforts that strengthen your skill base and improve your chances.

8. **Work on yourself, professionally, to match the work you began, personally, in Chapter One.** The two areas are in constant need of work, and they always touch each other.

9. Document key moments, ups and downs, with useful details for future reference. Lessons from past victories and defeats are a ready resource for making decisions of all kinds.

10. Join or form a small circle of colleagues who get together on a regular basis, to discuss common career or business issues. Its purpose is specific, and should be a referral source for other needs.

Consider these resources to add to your own:

- *300 Best Jobs Without a Four-Year Degree* by Michael Farr

- *Success* Magazine, **www.successmagazine.com**

- *Exploring Your Future, 200 Career Options* by Delmar Learning

- *The Everything Career Tests Book* by A. Bronwyn Llewellyn with Robin Holt, M.A.

- *Working Mother* Magazine, **www.workingmother.com**

- *Minority Rules. Turn Your Ethnicity Into a Competitive Edge* by Kenneth A. Roldan

- *Pink* Magazine, **www.pinkmagazine.com**

- U.S. Life Coach Association, **www.uslca.com**

- International Coach Federation, **www.coachfederation.org**

- **Career Development Services, www.careerdev.org**

- College Data, **www.collegedata.com**

- *We Are All Self Employed, The New Social Contract for Working in a Changed World* by Cliff Hakim

- *40 Best Fields for Your Career* by Michael Farr

- Magazine City (Trade and Professional Association Journals), **www.MagazineCity.com**

11. Execution

3

CHAPTER THREE:

The Organizational Dimension

Get Organized.

GET a handle on your organizational self, and put together a base of resources that can help you multiply your effectiveness and balance your weaknesses.

Many people think of organization in terms of pulling others together and getting things done. Actually, it is more basic than that. Organization, in its most basic sense, is developing a pattern of work that allows you to be resourceful, productive and effective on a consistent basis. Then as you raise the bar on your success, by whatever definition of success you choose, you will be better able to attract and utilize others to help you multiply that success.

The world is full of examples of highly talented, very bright people who fail to make a significant impact because they failed to make good decisions. Or they failed to establish a standard and a mechanism for accountability. Or they failed to hear useful criticism because they were too busy listening to the applause. Or they failed to keep an open door to new kinds of thinking which could help them adapt to change and keep moving forward. Getting organized means getting yourself, the processes and the people into place, to insure the greatest possible results.

1. Assess what kind of self-manager you are.

Decide what assets and liabilities you have in attracting and utilizing resources.

Just as we examined what you would need to do, to go further personally and professionally, the same kind of attention is needed to determine what you will need to do, to mobilize and manage your own skills and talents, as you attempt to attract other resources. What this means fundamentally is that your own practices and the mindset that they represent are key to your own effectiveness and your ability to incorporate and utilize others.

People who keep track of their commitments and obligations are more likely to fulfill them. Just as people who put their goals into writing are more likely to accomplish them, not because they are profoundly written, but because on paper they become a visible reference for action, review and reference. It might seem all too obvious, but people who operate on memory leave themselves open to the gaps that occur when memory fails. Keeping track of things is the most basic key to effective organization.

A few years ago, when there was lots of attention being paid to time management, I was finding that my most effective and productive clients were those who took good notes, kept up with them, and forged their own methods for getting things done. Those who were inconsistent in meeting deadlines or standards were those who were inattentive to small things, or those who undermined the importance of people around them who paid attention to small things. The problem was not time management. It was management.

No matter what career path you pursue, there are other people who can help you plan and go after your next level of achievement. But in order for them to help you, you need to have easy ways for them to plug in and do what they can do and are willing to do.

When a band starts to take its show on the road, the ideal situation is one where each member gets to focus on the music, the audience and the performance. How a tour plays out depends in many ways upon how the band does performance after performance. The musicianship is very important, but the process of moving the group from one performance to the next is in large part determined by leadership and cohesiveness within the group and good, reliable support. Management typically evolves with the success of the group, but the makeup of the people in the group can make it easier, harder, or impossible to put the resources together to help a group grow into its potential. No matter how they are portrayed in the public's eye, if the individuals bring habits that override the interests of the group, the group pays the price. Sometimes they break up. Sometimes they break down.

Good management requires the ability to coordinate ideas, energies and styles. Coordination becomes a more realistic possibility as members of a band make the commitment to supporting a process that respects the ordinary and routine work, and those who do it, that is essential for smooth operations and extraordinary results.

2. Consider your basic effectiveness.

It is important to recognize that the things that show up as unresolved issues or weaknesses in the Personal Dimension multiply themselves in the Organizational Dimension. How you feel about yourself will be reflected in how and how well you are able to incorporate the skills, ideas and differences others bring.

If you are often late for appointments, slow or lax in returning phone calls, fall behind or fail to meet established deadlines or disregard the budget or available funds on a regular basis, you may hereby consider yourself a piece of work, a person in need. You are standing in your own way, and any help others might provide would get lost in the chaos. If you are overburdened and are finding the busyness of business keeping you from being effective, your situation is likely one that can be resolved. When you have understandable ways of working, capable people can plug in and be productive, even if you can't quite tell them exactly what needs to be done. Deliberate, understandable work can be followed, coordinated and supported.

A good friend who loves the game of golf told me recently about having lost his swing. His concern, as he expressed it, was that he couldn't get useful help from a golf pro until he settled into a predictable, repeatable swing, even if the swing was not a good one. He said it wasn't so much that he just had a bad swing, but that it was "all over the place." He was encouraged that by the time he was telling me about it, he had at least gotten a regular swing established. So he then had a swing that could be described, analyzed and corrected. He went from no swing to a bad swing, and was happy about it.

As a non-golfer, I could not speak to the issue of his swing, or whether it was salvageable. But as a business consultant I have a clear memory of people I have known who had no discernable method to how they conducted business. It is clear to me that there are entrepreneurs who are operating without a swing, and until they settle into some kind of pattern, they will be virtually impossible to help.

Some entrepreneurs take advantage of lulls in business activity to assess where things are, while others use seasonal or other slow periods to slide into vacation time, not necessarily going on vacation but going into a nonproductive, vacation mode. All of this would be vigorously denied, by the way. The best hope for those in denial might be a not-too-damaging *Ahah!* moment, a slight bump into a wall, calling attention to the need to assess or change direction before new opportunities for solutions disappear.

If you don't follow through on ordinary tasks, meet deadlines and appointments, return phone calls promptly, keep good notes, and spend money according to some kind of plan, it is difficult to imagine how others will be able to help you in any substantial way. Before others can have the effect of fortifying or multiplying your stuff, there needs to be a way for them to attach themselves to something of substance. And, let's face it, aside from their capacity to help you multiply what you can already do, and fill the gaps in what you can't do, why else would you bring other people to the table?

One of the problems people have in going from a job to being self-employed is the unpredictability of it all. You could be working very effectively in a professional environment where you can afford to focus on just getting the work done. In a self-employment situation, especially where contract work is involved, you not only have to do the work, you have to land the business or account, and ultimately get paid. In many cases, these three things are handled separately. Getting paid may be the least of your qualifications or your experience, but nothing works if you aren't good at getting paid. And anxiety about getting paid can spill over into all sorts of seemingly unrelated things. If you are uncomfortable talking about and collecting money, you will need help, but you can't take yourself out of the role completely. Money is too important to making a living to allow you to let anxiety rule. Get better at dealing with it. Then get some help. After all, it's your career, your enterprise, your stuff.

So, no matter what vision you have for changing the world or taking it by storm, you cut yourself short if you don't give others a way of helping you take things from where they are, right now, to where you want them to be. Small-scale things might work out just fine, but breakthroughs to higher and higher levels require organization that begins with the visionary himself or herself. You have to help yourself first, and then let others help you.

3. Look at how, and how well, you communicate.

I keep running into examples of high-powered, fast-moving entrepreneurs who love spontaneity, and who like to brag about how overloaded they are. A common thread among them is their failure to appreciate the role of ordinary, unglamorous work and those who do it. They rarely admit these attributes, however. They often think they are models of support. Their communication is a key factor, because in too many situations too little thought is given to making sure those who carry out the mundane, day-to-day tasks are armed with the information and the sense of priority needed to function effectively. If it is hard for people in the trenches to know what's what, then it is virtually impossible to expect them to operate as the highly motivated, independent go-getters they are often asked to be.

The mistake too often made is to evaluate communications on how articulate people are, or how much charisma they seem to have, or how much they talk. The most basic communication need is to provide a clear set of goals, updates on the status toward the goals, and specific expectations and requirements of each person. Knowing what is going on and how each person fits are essential elements in building something that can function beyond your own energies. This basic communication is necessary for building a business, utilizing volunteers for a grass-roots organization, or launching a high-pressure, high profile career. Talent agents and campaign strategists are alike in that they cannot do their work effectively if they don't get straight, clear talk from those whose careers they are trying to launch. Candor and clarity are of the utmost importance.

4. Know what kind of decision-maker you are.

Nothing separates contenders and pretenders better than the way they make decisions. So, when we connect the information we gathered from the Personal Dimension several pages ago, we established a way of tracking ourselves in other dimensions as well. Organizational strengths are rooted in certain personal strengths.

Many people pride themselves in their reliance on spontaneity in their decision-making. Certainly, life would be far less interesting without it, but there are areas where careful consideration is key, and where a well-considered plan is something of great value. Hard choices, where there is much at stake, and where the answers are not always so obvious, require you to use your best thinking, incorporate the views of other trusted people, and make decisions that make sense. Sometimes "gut feelings" are all you have to work with, and in the final analysis, after the left-brain work is done, we trust ourselves to make the best decision that the available information and our intuitive sense suggest. The important thing is to use the limits of your thinking and the best available information when there is a lot at stake. And let reason be a regularly applied tool for you.

Most of the entrepreneurs and managers I have worked with or interviewed over the past 25 years would swear on a stack of Bibles that they weigh things carefully before making decisions. Unlike many of them, my friend and colleague Les Brown is honest. He would own up to his desire to throw caution and reason to the wind. He knows that he likes the spur-of-the-moment model when it comes to making decisions. And in some moments he would justify his penchant for spontaneity by pointing to a success or two that came in spite of his method.

When everything is said and done, though, I can usually produce a memorable list of missed or blown opportunities that better planning could have prevented. I usually win the argument, until he gets a new urge. But after working together for more than 30 years, I have *some* credibility, just not as much as I often think I have. My common refrain is, "Hey, it's your dream."

Let your decisions have their best chance of serving you by using a process that incorporates the following:

- **Get as much information as you can, proportional to the weight of the decision.**

- Weigh the options carefully, considering risk/benefit and cost/outcome issues.
- Get feedback from key people and take good notes.
- Sleep on it. Do not commit yourself before you reasonably have to.
- Be willing to change the decision, if it looks like it is the wrong one.
- Commit yourself and all available resources to assuring its success

Decisions make a difference, and how we make decisions plays a major part in the roles others can play in helping us multiply our stuff. People who are trying to support your venture or your cause need to have a sense of understanding, in order to be fully committed and fully functional. Communication and decision-making are two very important areas to understand in the organizational process. Style preferences have to be carefully considered, but ineffective uses of information of various kinds have stopped many a dream short of becoming reality. If your decision-making style works for you and your base of support, keep it. If not, give it up. How you decide, in general, could be far more important than any one decision you make. Ultimately, a solid, sensible process will pay dividends, again and again.

5. Determine who will help meet your needs

Figure out who can do, and will do, what on the road ahead.

In a previous section, we explored the issue of your base of support, the people who will be called upon to help you make, implement and evaluate decisions. No doubt, they will be needed to help you get on course and stay there, and to keep you grounded by putting the many successes and failures into perspective.

Once you know who is on your team for the long haul, you start to evaluate them on the particular skills they have, or are willing and able to learn, to help you reach your goals. And they might be key players in your evaluation process, who can help you when you need to add new people.

In addition to those people who are committed to you in a personal way, you will need to hire people to help you grow from stage to stage in various areas. Financial, legal, and management support are more critical in some fields than others. And very often, the free-wheeling traits that are important to being entrepreneurial work against the need to be good at screening, hiring, training and utilizing staff. When business owners seek to expand income or market share, they need to do a good job of hiring people who are capable and committed to following through on the unromantic details that make businesses work.

When Bobby expands his trucking business, or when Mike wants to put another sailboat or a larger one into the water, selecting the right people will be very important. Each will need to be able to trust that obligations are being met and that nothing is being done which might undermine the business. Bobby plans to use a consulting firm to help him screen and hire drivers. Then he will have to balance driving and overseeing others who will be driving for him. Carelessness is something owners can guard against when holding the reins, but they must rely on selecting good people and setting up practical and simple ways of keeping them accountable for those situations where they are not directly involved or in less control.

Bobby will have the advantage of his dad's experience and insights as he goes from solo entrepreneur to the head of a small team of drivers. His younger brother will also be able to help him sort things out and make good judgments. Captain Mike won't have similar family resources at his disposal, but he is in the early stages of business ownership. He is likely some years away from owning a fleet on the Caribbean, but the appeal of charter trips and his own experience as captain in someone else's fleet might be the inspiration for a move sometime in the future.

On the other hand, Keith found out who would help him build his barbering business and who would not when he expanded too quickly, adding a location across town, too far to give proper attention, and with people too new and unfamiliar to trust. After closing the extra shop and plotting a new course, he is going in a different direction, partnering with his wife, a cosmetologist, in a broader venture in a new and more attractive location than he was initially able to afford. Lessons learned. New opportunities emerge.

Get the input of people you trust. Parents might not know the inside information in a specific field or industry, but there is no substitute for family scrutiny in helping an aspiring athlete, scientist, fashion model, or pianist weigh offers from recruiters of various kinds. The same holds true for more conventional fields, where input from those you trust can help you weigh your options. The people in positions of trust, including coaches, teachers and mentors, can do a good job of helping parents and other supporters weigh options to help their loved ones make moves that make sense. Strong supporters with a history of involvement and a demonstrated concern in your career might be of greatest value by asking the tough questions, the ones that needed to be pondered, below the surface and beyond the ordinary.

8. Set up a process for effectively monitoring and evaluating your efforts.

You need a way to assure that you get the kind of feedback you need to manage your course and get results.

The great thing about plans is that they project a picture of the path you are taking that can be shared with everyone involved.

Planning serves as a reference point for making decisions and setting priorities, as well as providing ways to better coordinate usage of time, money and other resources. Plans are a centering tool for people with varying responsibilities, giving them a context for better understanding the importance of what they are doing and where things are headed. Whether it is for keeping volunteers involved or keeping staff focused, knowing the larger picture, beyond immediate responsibilities, is important for the level of buy-in that accompanies moving dynamically forward. Routine, ordinary work needs to be done well and on a timely basis.

The not-so-great thing about plans is that they can become either an excuse for inaction or the scapegoat for unsuccessful efforts. Plans actually have no value, except as they allow us to focus ideas, energies and resources on a specific course, and produce results. Planners sometimes confuse the situation by presenting a plan as something more. Others dismiss plans completely, because the intended results are not always reached, or because there is a false expectation of a crystal ball effect, that planning is useless because it somehow fails to provide guarantees. I hear freelance entrepreneurs and high-profile personalities bragging about how they like to make decisions on the basis of their gut-feelings. My own gut-feeling is that the successful ones have someone standing not-too-far away who is scrambling to put together a plan to bring the idea or project into focus and then into reality.

Several years ago, when consulting on a daily television show, we held reviews after every production. Our daily post-mortem, as we called it, gave an opportunity to assess how the production went and how it might be improved. And by doing it when the impressions were fresh in our minds, we could build in ways to avoid similar problems or to repeat things that went particularly well. We had a plan, and a way of reviewing our progress in small increments. Projects of many kinds can utilize a review immediately after being completed, to assess and decide how to improve efforts for the future.

The big thing about planning is what it can help you accomplish. If you get an opportunity to lay out a plan with a series of steps that can take you where you want to go, then give it a chance. Don't get caught up in some simplistic idea that the plan takes care of itself. A good plan is changeable and workable. So, if it works, work it. If it doesn't, change it so that it does.

* * * * * *

The thing about organization to keep in mind is that the better organized you are, the better or the easier it is for other people to understand and support what you do. This does not mean you have to be a great manager, but it is important that you appreciate what is involved and recognize what another manager or employee requires from you, to be effective.

Another thing to bear in mind is that nobody can help get you organized without your full participation. No matter how simple it looks when one of the morning shows matches someone with a personal organizer, to eliminate clutter and create order. They don't bother to follow up, and if they did, they would see how short a time it takes to re-create the clutter they tried to solve. If new patterns of thinking aren't created, old patterns of behavior and disorganization will reappear.

Careers take off all the time without the achiever having a sense of how to do what needs to be done in areas where they are either uncomfortable, uninformed or both. The key is to establish an understanding of what others are doing and be able to evaluate it, to see if it is working. And you also need to give helpers an understanding of what you are doing so that they can really help.

If you want to build a career that grows and lasts, the quality of the support you get will be very important. If your standards, habits and methods make management too difficult, you will spend far too much time and effort on a revolving door of staff and managers whose results are limited by your methods, but often blamed on theirs. ◣

Answers and Actions Needed:

1. **Get a good handle on your organizational habits and how you can strengthen them.** Get feedback from those who know you, personally and professionally, to help assess problems and opportunities for adding and utilizing people to expand your reach.

2. **Begin identifying who and what you are missing in your base of support, and what needs to be strengthened.** Who can and will help you fill the gaps, including paid professionals?

3. **Be willing to bring bright and talented people into your circle by showing a willingness to listen to dissenting opinions.** Are you one of those people who seeks input only to validate your own ideas? Don't let your ego push people away who might be very helpful to you.

4. **Structure your support.** Write your goals, core strategies, and ways you need people to help you broaden and strengthen your resources. Discuss your needs and ask people to help by playing the roles you have identified.

5. **Use your current base of support to enhance your resources and to attract others to your base.** Continue to add and strengthen your resources as your success and needs grow. Is the feedback something you are comfortable handling?

6. Meet periodically with your key supporters, perhaps alone but eventually as a group, to give updates and get feedback from them, for making decisions and weighing options. Is the feedback something you are comfortable handling? If not, dig back into Chapter One and work on the issues raised.

7. Make a commitment to getting the clutter out of your life. Is disorganization following you around? Use the feedback you get from supporters to get yourself on the right track.

8. Put together a workable evaluation process. It is one thing to write your goals, it is another to assure that you meet them. Since planning is important in getting people on board, then evaluating progress is important for keeping them focused, moving forward, knowing what is working and what is falling short.

9. Use your evaluation process to make decisions and determine priorities. Invest resources and make changes in accordance with the information that is revealed. Are you adaptable enough to change your plans as the information suggests? If not, you miss the real value of planning.

Consider these resources to add to your own:

- *Organizing from the Inside Out* by Julie Morgenstern

- International Virtual Assistants Association, **www.ivaa.org**

- *Goals, How to Get Everything You Want—Faster Than You Ever Thought Possible* by Brian Tracy

- *Network Journal,* **www.tnj.com**

- *The Art of Mingling* by Jeanne Martinet

- *7 Habits of Highly Effective People* by Stephen Covey

- *Skills for New Managers* by Morey Stettner

- *Ego Check, Why Executive Hubris Is Wrecking Companies and Careers and How To Avoid the Trap* by Mathew Hayward

- *What Got You Here Won't Get You There* by Marshall Goldsmith

- *Organization Smarts, Portable Skills for Professionals Who Want To Get Ahead* by David W. Brown

- *Thinking Inside the Box, The 12 Timeless Rules for Managing a Successful Business* by Kirk Cheyfitz

- *Execution, The Discipline of Getting Things Done* by Larry Bossidy and Ram Charan

4

CHAPTER FOUR:

The Promotional Dimension

1. Examine the lay of the land.

Determine the problems and opportunities you are likely to face in gaining and maintaining acceptance for your unique stuff.

In the Professional Dimension, we took a look at the field you are choosing, or have chosen, to get a handle on what kind of information, talent or expertise is required. In looking at the Promotional Dimension we concern ourselves with the marketplace, and all the issues we are likely to encounter in our efforts to establish ourselves.

Whether you realize it or not, whether it is your favorite area or not, you will probably need to spend some time being your own marketing "expert." Don't get carried away, looking at yourself as self-sufficient in that department. You will need help. Eventually, you will probably recognize that *you are the most qualified expert on your project, your venture, your goal, and your stuff.* Your expertise and the authority you have over your stuff require an intimate association with the areas that can affect your success. Committed attention brings about a whole new level of expertise for your effort.

We all need to spend time studying what is going on in the marketplace, as it applies to what we do or plan to do. And you don't have to be a marketing whiz to start figuring it out. What this means, basically, is that you need to have a good grasp of what is going on in your industry. It is in your interest to know who is finding success, and how that success is coming about. What new applications are emerging for your skill or talent? What examples of future opportunities do you see? Books, articles, the Internet, classes, conferences, association meetings, and interviews with industry professionals can be very important in gaining insights into what is working, where things are headed, and how the money and the opportunities are flowing.

When you know what is going on, what is being tried and with what success, you have some basis for determining your own direction. It's not all you'll need, but it is something. Not many years ago, very few of those who set their minds to becoming chefs would have considered the wide range of cooking applications which have exploded with changes in the American culture and media opportunities through cable television. The late Julia Child only touched the surface that Rachael Ray is digging into with a ton of books, television appearances and her own television shows. A couple of years ago I had never heard of Emeril Lagasse, but I found myself watching his "live" show, with his patented "Bam!" as he tosses seasoning on an entree in progress. All this is punctuated by the driving rhythm of drummer Doc Gibbs and the "Emeril Live Band."

Each of the cooking stars has his or her unique set of skills and styles. Sarah Moulton offers solid, functional tips and insights, while Giada De Laurentiis presents Italian fare with a special sense of style. Rachael Ray emphasizes 30-minute meals and restaurant hopping on a tight budget, and selling the whole culinary experience as big fun. Emeril has such a good time in his kitchen that it is not hard to imagine capturing some of his "Essence" taking hold on even a non-cook like me. Gerry "G" Garvin also cooks with a unique up-tempo energy, looking like he really enjoys expressing his own cooking dance. So, in an era when varying tastes and needs are involved, and media outlets find a range of options for inexpensively produced shows for various audiences, there appears to be lots of room for cooking, eating and drinking shows to exist and succeed.

There were many stages and changes along the path between Julia Child and Rachael Ray, including The Love Chef, Wolfgang Puck, The Cajun Chef and lots of others. Those who saw the trends developing in books, magazine articles and television segments, namely an interest in the how-to of classy cuisine, made their moves, and created programs and products to suit the growing consumer interest.

Unfortunately, if you have aspirations for reaching the highest levels in your industry, you probably need to know that you are unlikely to get there on a just-copy-the-others strategy. Defining what is special about you and what you offer is a critical, and often difficult, task. In facilitating workshops, I like to ask three questions that seem to take the wind out of people who have always looked at themselves only from the *inside out*. The questions are:

- **Who are you?**
- **What have you got?**
- **Why should anybody care?**

I remember the faces of the group where I first posed the questions in the late '80s. It was a marketing seminar for nonprofit organizations, and the faces showed a combination of indignation and puzzlement. I was pleased, and I am sure my sneering expression showed it. I needed to get their attention, because some of the organizations' very survival was at stake. In many cases, the sense of how they were viewed by others, including those who utilized and those who funded their services, needed a reality or sobriety check. I happily obliged.

If you don't start by doing your own homework, you will pay far more than necessary, and you'll probably be mystified by the razzle-dazzle, when you *do* need to bring a specialist on board. Just as no one is more of an expert *on you* than you are, no one knows better *where you are trying to go* with your stuff. So, if you can get a basic knowledge of what is happening in your industry, what people are buying or buying into, not only locally, but regionally and nationally (in some cases globally) as well, you will be in a much better position to succeed on your own path. Otherwise, you could end up moving quickly and efficiently down someone else's path.

2. Take a look at what you have to offer.

Examine your unique stuff and its value in the marketplace.

In the section in Chapter Two where we explored the Professional Dimension, we looked at your field of choice and the requirements to be successful at mastering the technical, professional and educational aspects of the field. We also explored in the Personal Dimension, Chapter One, the question of who you are and what you want. The thinking applied earlier is important now as we explore the promotional dimension. We need the earlier thinking, but we must now look at it differently. Now we are concerned with determining how your stuff gets applied and connected in the marketplace.

3. Get to know the competition.

Determine how you stack up.

Just as you want to have a good handle on what you have to offer, it is very important to know what the competition has to offer. When Alvin considers that the Jamaican jerk sauce he is bringing to grocery shelves and kitchens is not the only item of its kind in the mix, and that there are a number of exotic tastes competing for the public's palate and pocketbook, he knows that his homework needs to be more extensive. Otherwise, he might only concern himself with things like recipe refinement, quality control, bottling and related issues. He knows that positioning himself to sell sauce and build his brand will take much more.

You cannot afford to be unaware of what competitors are doing, but you cannot afford to be so preoccupied with the competition that you never fully develop what is uniquely yours. Being *mindful* of the competition is good. Being *preoccupied* with the competition is not.

4. Get to know and take care of your "customer."

Be committed to appreciating those who are in the market for what you offer.

No matter what field you are in, it is important to know who holds the keys to your successful entry. For someone on the corporate track, the customer is something different from that of an aspiring artist, a soft-drink maker or a hair-care product distributor. In fact, people who work in companies or organizations where they would like to move up are too often only concerned with positioning themselves when a particular job situation arises. Unfortunately, if you haven't put yourself in position to be considered for greater options, it is far more difficult to take advantage when opportunities arise. You need to view yourself as a continuously available resource, recognize the hiring process as the marketplace, and treat key people as your customers. Always. Not just when you are ready to make a move. Your door openers, mentors or other career supporters should be factored into your thinking and factored into your communications, so that your reputation is sustained and can create opportunities.

Not long ago, I had the opportunity to work with a sales organization seeking to do a better job of retaining customers. Addressing this common challenge makes good business sense. It is far less costly to expand the business you have had with past customers than to spend the time, money and energy reaching out for new customers in each sales cycle. But you have to know your customer. In fact, the more you know about those whose decisions can mean feast or famine, the better your chances of getting the feast.

Unfortunately, like many others, this company was looking for ways to attract and land new customers without knowing who their current customers were, what drew them, what turned them off, and what it would take to keep them engaged, happy, returning and referring. It is clear that marketing efforts are short-lived when they are not geared toward establishing a relationship as a valued part of making a sale.

No matter where you are in your career, or what field you are in, connecting with your customer, defined differently for different circumstances, can be invaluable. The people who help you get clients, get promoted, or get a foot in the door should be courted and acknowledged for the value they represent, if for no other reason than that they might be a future resource. Simple things often go a long way. As an interviewer, I have seen first-hand the impact of hand-written notes in helping separate and rank job candidates after competitive interviews. The good notes are hard to miss, and even harder to ignore.

5. Develop a plan for capturing your piece of the market.

Put together a basic strategy with details on how you will win with your stuff.

It can not be truthfully said that people without plans never succeed. In fact, there are many people, including some very successful ones, who like to dismiss the value of planning. In reality, many of the people who do very little planning of their own usually hire people who do enough to more than make up the difference. In the creative fields, especially, it is very chic to talk about spontaneity as a mode of functioning. My experience is that the more spontaneous the key personality is, the more structured the core people are. The sanity of the support person and the career of the spontaneous one could both be at stake.

By the same token, just as it is possible to be locked into spontaneity as a way of operating and suffer because of it, it is just as possible to be so locked into planning that fresh perspectives, new thinking and out-of-the-box thinking can be stifled. The promotional process needs fresh, innovative thinking as a way of carving out new ground, finding new angles for getting customers, or solving problems of various kinds where answers and solutions can seem very elusive.

In developing your business plan you decide how your business expects to make money, or make more money, and the plan is a vehicle for coordinating and evaluating action, priorities, decisions and overall effectiveness. Just as your business plan expresses a financial overview of how resources will be used and revenues generated, your marketing plan expresses how you plan to approach, land and retain customers. By deciding that a particular approach to past customers or a certain list of prospective customers will be your top priority, you will be setting the framework for a whole series of actions, assignments, and energies to be put forward. You will be putting into effect a strategy, which takes into account capabilities, pricing, promotional tools, targeted outreach and other issues. Your working plan gives you a way to see where you are at any point in time, and what needs to be done to be more successful.

6. Get the word out.

Let the world know about what you've got and why it has value.

When all is said and done, the real promotional challenge is to get the word out, to the right people, in the right way, so that your opportunities can be maximized. In an edition of the "60 Minutes" news show on CBS, New England Patriots' quarterback Tom Brady told how his father made him known to college football programs. According to Brady, his father sent out videos of his high school accomplishments to several college football coaches, because his son was receiving far less attention than the elder Brady felt was deserved. His promotional pack landed on the desks of several NCAA Division I-A coaches, those at the larger, elite level, and one of them responded with a phone call that led to a scholarship for young Brady.

After a moderately successful college career, playing at the University of Michigan, and modest assessments by NFL scouts, Brady was a late pick in the draft by the New England Patriots. But it wasn't until an injury occurred to the starting quarterback that he was cast into the national spotlight. After leading his team to three Super Bowl victories in a four-year period, he is seen as one of the best quarterbacks in today's game.

His accomplishments at the professional level make it worth noting that if Brady had gone unnoticed or unrecognized in high school, and had he not gotten a college scholarship to a major college, his love for the game might have landed him on a family room couch rooting for his favorite team. Lots of people who have watched Brady play can thank his dad for putting together that video and sending it to coaches across the country. Getting noticed is all it's cracked up to be.

In a completely different set of circumstances, Spanish painter Salvador Dali might have enjoyed much less success and a more modest lifestyle, but for the efforts of his wife Gala, whom it is said by his biographers was very knowledgeable of and well connected to the art world. Her expertise in getting his work recognized and received helped him avoid the "starving artist" life that has accompanied many art icons. Dali established a unique and intriguing style. His painting reflected a high standard, and thanks to his collaboration with his "other half," he lived life at the same standard.

The prominence of Picasso's work in the United States is attributed to a major New York showing of his work in the '20s. The right art dealer, connected with collectors who want to see their own fortunes grow with the artist's rise, can make a difference in the exposure an artist is able to receive, and the impact the artist is able to make, not only on the viewing public, but on other artists.

Picasso was able to influence tastes and attitudes about art and inspire other artists to incorporate his influences into their work.

7. Deliver what you promise.

Make sure you take each opportunity seriously.

Tom Brady's dad and his zeal for his son's career could not have covered an inability to play. Being solid at your craft is critical, but there are talented people going unnoticed in all kinds of places, in all kinds of fields, for lack of an effective way to find someone or some way to make good things happen in their careers. What is critical is making sure that the professional standards you develop to get you inside the door are executed in a way that can keep you inside the door. Dali's wife could not have used her connections and her know-how, if her husband's work did not deliver at the galleries.

Les Brown once told me about a situation he faced as he arrived at the site for a speech he was brought in to deliver, following an extensive publicity campaign. When he arrived at the location, staff people with the sponsoring organization began to offer apologies for the low turnout, feeling embarrassed at the results of their last-minute efforts to get the word out.

The event's sponsor was prepared to cancel the speech, since there was only a handful of people in the auditorium, which could seat hundreds. They would chalk up the experience to poor planning, pay Les, and forget the whole thing. The sponsor was surprised when Les said there were two issues of credibility at stake, the sponsor's and his own. Convincing the sponsor's representative that they should proceed, Les made his presentation as planned and began to notice that by proceeding with the doors open, several unexpected passersby heard him from the hallways and began to take seats. In the end, several dozen people came into the auditorium for the presentation, and several signed up as volunteers for the organization's new program. Also in attendance was the head of another organization who happened by. She had heard of Les, but had never seen him in person. She liked the presentation, and in a matter of days booked him for one of her organization's national meetings.

You never know who is listening to your message when you are speaking, and you never know who is watching you, even when you're not speaking. According to Brown, the woman who hired him was won over by the time and attention he gave to the small audience, as well as his presentation itself. His was a good example of a commitment to the audience, who had every right to expect him to make his presentation. After all, that is why they, if only a handful, attended.

* * * * * *

When you know what you want to do and are prepared to do it, and you get the support you need to carry it out, what remains is to find a position for it in the marketplace. It is not enough to be good at what you do, to make a great impact with it. You need to have an effort underway that can factor the view of your stuff from the *outside in,* not just from the inside out. So, if your efforts are bolstered by a team who can help you weigh options and make decisions that will get you highly recognized and highly regarded, you give yourself the best chance for ongoing success.

Reputation rules. You can take your chances with those who dismiss their inroads and take chances on the public's short memory, or rely on the hope that arrogance will go under the radar, but it is a gamble that threatens the kind of success that is ongoing and repeatable in other potentially more rewarding areas.

Actions and Answers Needed

1. Do you have a sense of what you have to offer to the marketplace, and what distinguishes you from others?

2. Confer with supporters and available insiders and determine a basic game plan for establishing and strengthening your identity, your brand.

3. **Are you a good advocate for yourself?** Good, crisp thoughts are needed that articulate what is special about your stuff, to help you and your advocates establish inroads.

4. **Are you an effective networking resource?** Get used to interacting and establishing key relationships, which can create avenues to the next level and beyond.

5. **Make your auditions, interviews, tryouts, shows or presentations testing grounds for your stuff.** Each gives an opportunity to learn about yourself and how the marketplace responds.

6. **Are you a good closer?** At the higher levels in some fields, it is agents, headhunters and other representatives who get you into important doors. Your job is to close what somebody else has opened. Your job is to finish what has been started.

7. **Give your customer a reason to come back.** Deliver what you promise, what is expected, and something more, to leave a lasting impression.

Consider these resources to add to your own:

- *Persuasive Business Proposals, Writing To Win More Customers, Clients, and Contracts* by Tom Sant

- *We Are All Self Employed, The New Social Contract for Working in a Changed World* by Cliff Hakim

- *Knock 'em Dead 2007, The Ultimate Job Search Guide* by Martin Yate

- *Brand Hijack, marketing without marketing* by Alex Wipperfurth

- *The New Job Security, Five Strategies To Take Control of Your Career* by Pam Lassiter

- *According to Kotler, The World's Foremost Authority on Marketing Answers Your Questions* by Philip Kotler

- *Network Journal,* **www.tnj.com**

- *The Art of Mingling* by Jeanne Martinet

- *Promoting Yourself, 52 Lessons for Getting To the Top...and Staying There* by Hal Lancaster

5

CHAPTER FIVE:

Business
Perspectives

MUCH of what has been written in earlier sections focuses on individual pursuits, including those of the entrepreneur. Yet there is a larger context for looking at this book's applications in business situations, and they are explored in this chapter. The paradigm of looking at things from a personal perspective parallels looking at businesses from within. Knowing the history of efforts tried and failed, the company's strengths, weaknesses and other more specific traits, its vision for the future and other aspects of the company's stuff are just as important for a company's prospects as they are for those of an individual. So, we return to the notion of looking at things from the *inside out*.

1. Get a clear picture of the company and what it has to offer.

Take a good inventory of company assets and liabilities, especially human ones.

Whether we are looking at auto detailers or auto dealers, each company has its unique view of itself and its unique needs and resources. The same is true for Captain Mike and his sailing excursion venture, as he attempts to use his sailing knowledge, his joy in sharing the experience, and the boat itself to solidify the business and enjoy life on the water. Mike doesn't have many of the headaches that large companies have, but he still has to sell his service, maintain a crew, meet monthly obligations, and suffer the ups and downs of his industry. Money is money, no matter what business is involved. So, even as he celebrated his second month as owner, Mike was looking past the glamour of the sunset and paying a lot more attention to routine, unromantic details. The captain will have a few headaches of his own, but he is passionate about what he is doing, and that passion will offset many of the headaches of owning his own business. So, going from operator to owner could have a great deal of promise for Mike and his sailing venture, with the kind of attention that allows a dream to be realized, sustained and expanded.

Most companies and their key people don't need to be asked to look at the world from *inside out*. It happens naturally. Unfortunately, many companies are reluctant to look at their weaknesses when they are doing an internal assessment. And all too often they treat their vision as something that serves more of a symbolic role than a practical one. It can be much like the business plans that startup entrepreneurs develop when looking for loans, grants or investments. When your business plan is not built into the ways you do business, you miss out on its ability to help you make decisions that will drive the activities, resources and business priorities. When the business plan is a clean document, with no notes, underlined phrases, or corrections in the margins, it says a lot about the company and its commitment to evaluating and ensuring progress toward good outcomes. The plan itself is not the key: the use of the company's best thinking, to gauge progress and create accountability, is the key. The business plan, if it is a good one, provides a good way to look at the company from within, while taking the needs of the outside world into account.

When a company knows its strengths and weaknesses, its history of success and failure, its unique problems and opportunities, and the edge it can use to attract and maintain customers and strategic alliances, it has a wealth of information on which to maintain and build business.

2. Decide the direction the company will be headed.

When the late Bill Williams, the founder of Glory Foods, was still tied up in the details of running my favorite restaurant, he was carrying its weight into his new food products venture. Bill had made the Marble Gang a popular restaurant, but after more years as a restaurant owner than he would have liked, his role as CEO of Glory began to take over. He was excited about the prospects for the new company. One slow night in the restaurant, we sat in my regular corner and talked about where his business was going, and he smiled, reflecting on the cities and grocery stores his popular pre-cooked side dishes were getting into. I had not heard about the frozen food line, the expansion from canned goods, so I got a good sense of how big things were getting. I also got a sense of how much of a drain the restaurant had gotten to be on the far more explosive, new business. Bill said he wanted to sell the restaurant, but that he also wanted the new owner to be successful, continuing the legacy he had started.

Although Bill only lived a few years after he sold the Marble Gang, Glory Foods has continued its growth, getting into more cities, more grocery stores, more shelves and more homes. Unfortunately, the Marble Gang did not make it. After changing hands a few times, the once-prominent restaurant closed.

3. Determine what resources will be needed to succeed.

When companies know themselves thoroughly they stand a much greater chance of utilizing their resources to full advantage. They also know what they do not have, if they are honest. The biggest difference between lagging behind and moving ahead could rest on how well needs are identified and weighed. When a good, honest review has been taken, there is opportunity to face the needs squarely.

Needs to move forward vary with the company and the industry. They can include staff shortages, unpredictable cash flow, outdated technology, or virtually any number of possibilities. One common need I see is an absence of training to meet basic functions. Too much emphasis is placed on the effort to hire better, with the assumption that the learning curve for new people will take care of itself. Smaller companies to a greater extent, but companies in general, place too little value on routine, unexciting training that ensures continuity. By comparison, many companies will spend substantial training dollars to bring a new technology on board. But cross training to assure continuity in operations is too often overlooked or underused.

Most companies can also benefit by more effective, routine communication and coordination, keeping common attention on common objectives, and avoiding some of the gaps and duplication that happen even under the best of circumstances. The needs can be wide ranging, but the process for identifying and dealing with them needs to be simple, direct and open.

Business owners who are honest about their needs, who will listen to the feedback from knowledgeable sources, and then factor that feedback into their thinking give themselves greater opportunities to succeed. Just as professionals must have a keen awareness of what they need to succeed, businesses and other organizations need the same kind of awareness and a commitment to reaching out to get it. And very often the most underutilized resources are those closest at hand. Creating an environment that is friendly to internal feedback can be very important, if the aim is to move things to the next level or into a new arena. Unfortunately, there is often a huge gap between saying you want candid feedback and setting a tone where it is more likely to take place. Staff and other insiders can smell pretense a mile away.

4. Make the commitment to getting the resources you need.

Often the resources needed to step up are beyond the company's immediate grasp. Technology upgrades, additional staff, or more available credit might require that they, too, be phased in over a period of time. Determine a strategy to incorporate your needs into your plans, so that you can work, step by step, toward meeting the needs. The commitment is key. Once you have made it a necessity, and not an option, you will have raised the level of urgency to get things moving. The desire to drive up sales, market share or profitability must be matched by a clear and obvious commitment throughout the business to get there.

Sometimes the resource in greatest need is leadership. When you make the commitment to meeting the company's needs, get as clear as you can about the roles you and others are playing, and can play, to maximize business potential. Investors, partners and key operations people need to help examine roles and expectations periodically, in light of company needs, and make the necessary adjustments.

5. Identify and build upon your uniqueness.

By looking at your business from the *outside in*, you gain a perspective that improves the chances for creating a match between you and your customers. Just as you want to be clear about where you are headed, you need to be equally clear about what sets you apart from other companies. This does not mean being preoccupied with the assets or unique offerings other companies have, but it does mean being aware of them.

Your stuff, from a business perspective, includes all the special things that might allow you to attract and retain customers and grow your business. It might include location or ambience, pricing, level of quality, special features, or the breadth of products or services. Or it might include a special way of accommodating customers. Whatever you have to offer that is unique or rare, and appreciated by customers, might have the potential to become your primary inroad to your customer base and to establish your identity in the marketplace.

Once you have identified your package of assets, use them to attract and retain customers. And don't tamper with or weaken those things that represent your stuff. Keep them and strengthen their value as assets by a consistent standard in which they are offered.

6. Know and value your customer.

When you know almost as much about your customer as you do about your business, you have a world of options. You have the ability to offer what your customer wants, if you know the tastes, the spending habits, the needs, the whereabouts, the lifestyle and other aspects of those who buy your products. You have a wealth of information on which you can make decisions.

Knowing your customer gives you insights you can use for building ongoing relationships. And knowing your customer introduces you and your staff in practical ways to the economics of valuing the customer. Customer retention and referrals are far more efficient ways of building a business than advertising and other conventional ways of getting customers. Unfortunately, customer retention is not an easy proposition.

In many companies customer retention comes from the perspective that the customer matters when customer dissatisfaction arises. My study of customer service in the mid 90s led me to a wide range of conclusions, many of which represent common sense, if not common practice. Customer care comes from customer value. And as attractive as it might be to promise something special in the way of customer service, it is not really a good idea, if you don't have the intention and the means to deliver. Avoid the dreaded disappointment (anticipointment, if you will) that leads to customer bashing and other negative business chatter. Don't pretend. If you really want to make your customer-care strategy part of your business identity, set the wheels in motion to get a quality program into place. It starts with leadership from the top, but it really needs real attention at the bottom, in the trenches, to assure that ideas and values that reach customers in practical, measurable, noticeable ways.

7. Develop a reputation for reliability.

One of the ways to distinguish your company from the field of also-rans is by establishing a reputation not just for being good, but for being reliable. Everyone starts out intending to be reliable. Just ask them. Unfortunately, the road to business failure is paved with good intentions. Nobody sets out to establish inconsistency as a way of doing business. But it happens. By adding locations prematurely or by hiring people too soon or too casually, standards suffer. The difference between being reliable and being unreliable can be seen in the level of detail that can only be assured through systematic attention to detail.

When the restaurant serves one of your favorite dishes, it can be very disappointing if the preparation is inconsistent. It could be a dessert or an entrée. If a hot dish arrives lukewarm or the seasoning is off the mark, it can spoil the dining experience, and leave you feeling lukewarm about the restaurant. The issue is not always a lack of friendliness or slow service or the general taste of food. When it comes to the very specific taste and texture of food that restaurants use to win customers, it can't be sometimes. It has to be, or appear to be, always.

The program you set up to assure a repeatable pattern of quality is the only way to know that all the bases are covered, or to know when and where a snag occurs. Quality systems don't always prevent errors. They identify or catch errors, so that they can be corrected. If your company can establish a reputation as reliable, it will become a major asset in helping to establish or strengthen your business identity, and attract customers.

8. Let the world know what you have and why they need it.

When you have identified the valuable features your company offers and the benefits for customers doing business with you, you have a beginning piece for establishing your position in the marketplace. What you will need is a core strategy and a full-fledged marketing plan that will take you to the next level. Your marketing plan should be dynamic, changing to accommodate new developments and new information, so that it can help in your decisions regarding pricing, where and how your products or services will be offered, the appropriate promotional tools to be used, and a whole range of related matters.

So, once the strategy and action plans are in place, you set out to let the world know what you've got and why they should care. And you never stop adjusting your focus to fit the changing demand. The simplest thing, though not always the easiest, is to put your business in position to attract customers, satisfy them, and add new customers until you reach your capacity to deliver effectively. Then you improve capacity to continue growing.

* * * * * *

When you know what you want your business to do and be, the question is: How are you going to take it there? Starting with an internal review and incorporating impressions from the market-place, you establish a basic strategy to address your needs and take advantage of opportunities. By addressing internal needs and limiting any downsides in attracting and maintaining business, you allow energies to be devoted to strengthening and expanding your customer base. It is important to establish a reputation for providing a consistently good product or service, which can go a long way toward attracting and retaining customers. Going the extra mile assures that customers are valued in the company, reaping benefits in repeat business and referrals. And as you develop your customer base and add new customers, stay on track with standards that helped create opportunities in the first place. ◄

Answers and Actions Needed

1. **Conduct a candid review of your business, including its history, mission, capabilities, or original intent, and the problems and opportunities it is likely to face.**

2. **Can your current way of thinking and operating take you where you want to go?** Determine what resources and priorities are needed to get you to your goal.

3. **Develop a written plan to focus your energies, ideas and expertise where they can produce the greatest results.** Have you included strategies you will use to maximize your management and marketing opportunities? The Small Business Administration, the Chamber of Commerce, and other not-for-profit and for-profit organizations can help.

4. **Is there a solid customer-care attitude present, even among those who have little customer contact?** How will you assure that customer value gets built into or maintained as a company attitude?

5. **What will you do to assure that the standards you set for yourself and your company are maintained as your staff grows or changes?**

6. **Measure the results of all your efforts, to get a good sense of how to compare past, present and future efforts.**

7. **Make sure everyone is on board. Partners, investors, managers and overall staff need to be brought into the discussion of future expectations.** Hold meetings and use other forums for feedback to get a solid sense of a team mindset.

8. **Rally your troops. Give your business and all its contributors the best chance to succeed by focusing energies in practical ways.** Give them a basis for a full, meaningful effort.

9. **Recognize and reward your people for effort and success. Does everyone know that a good effort of various kinds is valued?** Does achievement get appropriately recognized? Create moments to acknowledge, specifically and generally, when great contributions have been made.

10. **Look for joint-venture or strategic-alliance opportunities. Smaller companies, especially, can extend their reach dramatically by aligning themselves where there is mutual value and a written, framework for working together.**

Consider the following resources to add to your own:

- Small Business Administration, www.sba.gov

- *Persuasive Business Proposals, Writing to Win More Customers, Clients, and Contracts* by Tom Sant

- *Ego Check, Why Executive Hubris Is Wrecking Companies and Careers and How To Avoid the Trap* by Mathew Hayward

- *The Big Book of Small Business, You Don't Have To Run Your Business by the Seat of Your Pants* by Tom Gegax

- *Entrepreneur* Magazine, www.entrepreneur.com

- *Black Enterprise* Magazine, www.blackenterprise.com

- *Inc.* Magazine, www.inc.com

- *Fortune Small Business* Magazine, www.fsb.com

- *Business Week* Magazine, www.BusinessWeek.com

- *The Wall Street Journal*, www.wallstreetjournal.com

6

CHAPTER SIX:

Non-Profit Perspectives

ALTHOUGH many organizations are slow to realize it, surviving and thriving in the not-for-profit world can be every bit as challenging as it is in the for-profit sector. So, having a keen awareness of an organization's identity is a key starting place for raising friends and raising funds. Having worked in the public and nonprofit sectors prior to hanging out my shingle as a consultant, I learned the importance of courting legislative favor and establishing a niche in the philanthropic marketplace as keys to an agency's or an organization's survival.

1. Get a handle on the problems and opportunities your organization faces.

Those who understand the challenges and organize themselves to obtain financial and other resources have an inside track to longevity and effectiveness that others do not enjoy. Good causes too often are matched with little beyond good intentions, and their constituents suffer.

A few years ago, I almost had the opportunity to work on an effort to "turn the corner" for Atlanta's Morris Brown College. The small college, with a solid legacy in African-American education, was facing a loss of its accreditation. I was asked to come in by the newly appointed president, whom I had worked with successfully in an uphill situation more than 25 years earlier. It looked like a great opportunity to do something good, and I was excited. Unfortunately, the college was up against a complex set of problems, different but related. The new president had a short period of time to convince the accreditation committee that he could turn the situation around, and after spending a day on campus, meeting with him and some members of his team, I was convinced that he could do what was required. Unfortunately, the review committee did not agree. Accreditation was withdrawn. Challenges in financial aid management and other areas were seen as too great to extend accreditation on a provisional basis. A new and capable president notwithstanding, the committee voted no. I like to think of myself as someone who can see beyond appearances, and I think I saw great opportunity at Morris Brown, given the right leadership and other key resources. Many of the challenges in private higher education reflect scenarios in the nonprofit sector in general. You have to make the case for your value, and you need to be able to martial the resources to pull you through hard times. All of this takes time, and you don't always get the time you need.

The student body dropped to a virtual handful, as the college did its best to hold things together. Alumni and friends in Atlanta and around the country came to Morris Brown's aid, but the accreditation issue hung heavily overhead. No doubt, the recent few years have been tough. Here's hoping that this college has been able to find some lessons in the hard times that will serve them in the future, keeping a proud and important legacy intact.

2. Continue to strengthen the organization's capabilities.

Being good at what you do is as important for organizations as for individuals.

Several years after completing a consulting project for a human services agency, I got a chance to talk with an administrator who was still with the agency, but in a more substantial management role, some 20 years later. When she told me that a report I had submitted was still on file, and was still a reference document for decisions the agency makes, it was flattering, especially considering the number of years. Not long afterwards, I took the opportunity to meet with staff, review the agency's current challenges and make some recommendations that might help them in this new era. The challenges were far different after 20 years, but overall the task was just as great. One of the agency's strongest assets, I said in my follow-up report, was the heightened level of knowledge and commitment of staff. They knew why they were there, and they had the skill set and the mindset to be effective. The why makes the how a lot easier.

The public sector has its challenges as well. In the '70s I worked as a legislative aide, responsible for scrutinizing the annual budget for a city's development department. Each fall, the dance began with hearings, getting the departmental spin, checking with other information sources, and finding holes in the budget and the surrounding rhetoric. Some departmental personnel made it tough, others made it interesting, and a few were good enough at reading the political winds and adjusting their proposals to create a budget that would speak to various interests.

Public agencies at all levels have their own objectives. Some of them are driven by zeal to accomplish something of substance, while others are driven by partisan or ideological considerations. Environmental protection, child welfare advocacy, highway safety, drug abuse enforcement, and many other programs attract "true believers." Yet it is not at all uncommon to have the desire to reach or maintain a high standard collide with the need to please an important constituent or group. A common name for the collision is "bureaucratic red tape." Many agencies prevent disaster in small, ordinary ways because dedicated professionals refuse to hurry approval on such things as unsafe building plans or unhealthy kitchen conditions. The credit is rarely forthcoming for maintaining such standards, but condemnations for failing to do so become front-page news. Public agencies of all kinds need to make the case for having the funding, the guidelines and other resources to do what the public expects, because public expectations don't decrease when budgets are reduced.

3. Determine where you can do the most good.

See if you can match your desire with a need.

In the aftermath of Hurricane Katrina, the Gulf Coast in general and New Orleans in particular took such a great blow that in the retrospectives done by the news media on the first anniversary, there appeared to be so little done that the "feel good" stories seemed vastly outweighed by what needed to be done. The gaps in service, the bureaucratic harshness and ineptitude, along with the combination of arrogance and ignorance at various government levels left very little for anyone in the public or private sector to brag about. The sad fact is that New Orleans is a unique American disaster story, not simply because of the damage of the levies and the destruction of homes, neighborhoods, and families. The sheer magnitude of the physical damage and the broader magnitude of the emotional damage through the crass displacement of a half-million residents make for a situation that is ripe for a massive rebuilding effort that reaches far beyond new levies and new housing. And inaction added insult to injury. This complex, multi-layered problem needs public money, innovation and energy from all levels. Philanthropic, governmental, corporate, bi-partisan, and long-term leadership is what is really called for, to counter a critical mass of negatives. There appears to be plenty of opportunity for real work to be done, away from the spotlight, ripe for a hero or a heroine, maybe a few of each.

One bright New Orleans story among so many dismal ones is the creation of "Musicians' Village." This special project of Habitat for Humanity, in its collaboration with native New Orleans musicians Branford Marsalis and Harry Connick, Jr., is building a multi-block area of houses for musicians. Considering the role music has played in the cultural life of New Orleans, "Musician's Village" speaks directly to the notion of a new New Orleans, grounded in well-established traditions. It is a small project, considering the scope of the need, but it offers a light for looking forward. Situated in the "Musicians' Village" is the Ellis Marsalis Center for Music, which allows the senior Marsalis, his sons, and many others to contribute to the musical future of New Orleans and, thereby, the world.

4. Follow your heart. But use your head.

When Oprah Winfrey announced the opening of her school in South Africa, she described it as a long-time dream. Using her own money to build it, Oprah's leadership academy is evidence of her commitment to creating opportunities for aspiring girls who are eager to accomplish great things. The Oprah Winfrey Leadership Academy for girls is almost sure to distinguish itself as a place for education and empowerment, with Oprah's circle of influential "friends" and her proven ability to leverage her show, her audience, her experience, and her passion to make things happen. As the school develops its educational foundation, there are opportunities at an even higher level that Oprah and her potential pool of distinguished faculty will be able to bring to bear. Through the opportunities for virtual instruction via on-line courses, live teleconferencing, floating seminars and summer programs, the Leadership Academy could be in position to have an even more global impact. Places like Chicago, Baltimore, London, New York, Houston, Los Angeles, New Delhi and New Orleans could be running courses at the same time, using educational and developmental programs that speak to her passion. There would also be the potential for offering courses or programs for women, along with girls, beyond South Africa, as well as for men and boys. In a world of global communication, technology can provide information and learning in ways we might never have envisioned, at lower costs than past models would have required.

* * * * * *

When people in the non-profit world know their agency's history, its mission, and its strengths and weaknesses, they can apply their energies and resources to maximum advantage. Building and strengthening professional capabilities, organizing to make the best use of their personnel and volunteers, and reaching out to attract, utilize and sustain resources can help them succeed with those they serve, directly and indirectly.

The principle of working from within or from *inside out* provides opportunities to see that there is consistency with the mission, so that programs and priorities express the original intent. On the other hand, looking from the *outside in* lets you see yourself in a way that allows you to adjust what you are doing to meet a pressing need. Knowing what else is being done, and identifying needs that are not being met, gives insights into how you can and should adjust, to maintain value and support.

The world of public and non-profit work is so vast, and often poorly understood, that it never ceases to be important to keep the general public, supporters, and those who benefit directly from your work well apprised of the challenges you face and the breakthroughs that occur. ◄

Answers and Actions Needed

1. Take a good, hard look at your organization from *inside out*, examining its mission, current programs, resources and needs. Is it doing what is expected? What does it need to do its job more effectively?

2. Does the organization, with its programs, services and resources, reflect future goals and plans? If not, determine what changes you will need to make to get on the right track.

3. Engage staff, volunteers, advisors and policy makers in the process of determining future plans, and in reaching out for additional resources.

4. Take a look at things from the **outside in**. How do service users, donors, affiliates, policy makers, media, the general public, and competing agencies view your organization and its role?

5. Incorporate feedback from the outside, to give the organization validity in the marketplace. Do the general public and key constituents understand and appreciate the value of what you provide?

6. Are natural supporters or constituents armed with the information needed to advocate in your organization's or agency's behalf?

Consider these resources to add to your own:

- *You Don't Need a Title To Be a Leader* by Mark Sanborn

- *Why Non-Profits Fail; Overcoming Founder's Syndrome, Fundphobia and Other Obstacles to Success* by Stephen R. Block

- *Skills for New Managers* by Morey Stettner

- *Managing Government Employees, How To Motivate Your People, Deal with Difficult Issues, and Achieve Tangible Results* by Stewart Liff

- *The Non-Profit Board Answer Book, Practical Guidelines for Board Members and Chief Executives* by Robert C. Andringa and Ted W. Engstrom

- Volunteer Match, **www.volunteermatch.org**

- 1-800-Volunteer, **www.volunteermatch.org**

7

CHAPTER SEVEN:

Career Transitions

In an era in which more and more people are looking for ways to express themselves through their work, the means to that end has been through career changes, even dramatic ones, often later in life. Deciding to live one's "passion" can mean the change from an ordinary but predictable life to an unusual and less predictable one. The transition itself is important and should not be underestimated. I hear people discussing retirement nowadays as a vehicle for finally doing what they always wanted to do. Reaching retirement at a younger age and in good health can be the basis for doing something really satisfying.

1. Take a look at yourself first. Be sure of where you are going and why.

The process for making an effective career transition is the same as that outlined in Chapter One. You first need to take a hard look at who you are, what you have to offer, what matters most to you, and what obstacles you are likely to have to overcome, to get to where you want to go. And the process for examining yourself should not be undertaken alone. Feedback from those who want to see you succeed is invaluable, and very often eye opening.

With the retirement of "baby boomers," the largest wave of second-career professionals is emerging, looking to achieve a greater degree of career satisfaction or financial security or both. Some of the second career or new career people (some have been around more than once) will be starting their own businesses, including ventures in fields where they have worked. Others will be pursuing long-time dreams of business ideas where they feel they can put their energies and talents to work and make a profit.

While some people will be making career transitions with plans to earn money as a primary focus, others will be looking to use their experience and expertise to make a social impact. A recently retired teacher I met wants to volunteer in school as a tutor. She has been asked to apply for a paid position, but says she specifically looks forward to working with children for free, to make a contribution under circumstances that would allow her to feel even better about her work by removing money from the picture. Similarly, an evening news story recently profiled a group of doctors who are volunteering at urban health clinics on short but regular shifts, wanting to re-commit themselves to seeing patients in a situation where money and managed care issues would not need to be considered.

2. Examine the field and its requirements.

Once you have completed the process of evaluating yourself, gotten a sense of what contribution you want to make and what hurdles you need to overcome, it is important to pay attention to the requirements in the Professional Dimension, pointed out in Chapter Two, where big mistakes are often made. Expertise can be the basis for a competitive edge, but new entrepreneurs often operate with an expectation that their expertise will carry the day. It is very important to read, study and talk with experienced people and your career supporters who can give you insights into the new arena and your best chances for success. I am often surprised at how easy some people think it is to run a business successfully. After all, looking at all the businesses that are out there, how hard could it be? Considering all the businesses that are no longer out there, it is worth noting that maintaining and growing a business can be pretty hard.

Kitchen experience or expertise does not guarantee a successful catering business or a successful restaurant. What is needed to go along with successful culinary experience is attention to customer tastes and demands, staffing needs, licensing, location, layout, purchasing, menu, staffing, pricing, and many others areas. The move from cook or chef to caterer has steps to be climbed, just as the move from caterer to restaurant owner does. And climbing the steps from a simpler to a more complex venture takes know how, homework, careful decision making, and some hard work. All of these elements contribute to success, and knowledgeable people can make a successful transition into a new field most easily if they *know* what they *don't know* and are willing to learn.

3. Find out what new knowledge, skills and resources will be needed.

The problem with many career transitions is that a little learning can be dangerous. Some chefs are better suited for the role of caterer than the multi-dimensional role as restaurateur. Caterers don't necessarily have a smooth road, but it is certainly less complex. So, if you have a successful cooking background and the next level or the dream level you aspire to is a successful restaurant, commit yourself to a process of learning all you can to help you evaluate what you will need to successfully make your move.

Retailers might start with kiosks or special-occasion sales to test their buy-and-sell instincts. The things you learn about yourself as you learn about the field are invaluable, especially if your role in that field is to be different. Often managers think they know what owners know. Sometimes it takes the heat of direct experience to find out the difference. The transition from a back burner, part-time role to a front burner, full-time one is also a hard one for many to see. Doing something in your spare time has little of the pressure that comes with a project or venture that dominates your calendar. Starting a venture in retirement requires that you take time and effort into account, to avoid a lot of frustration and disappointment that might otherwise occur.

4. Give yourself an edge.

You might be new to a prospective field but you owe it to yourself to find and use your strengths in ways that can help create a demand for what you bring to the table. When Les Brown and I get together to conduct training for aspiring public speakers, there is always a group of trainees interested in using their speaking talents to advance their existing careers. It makes sense. Some want to be booked, to make money through speaking fees, but others are seeking to enhance their professional recognition and distinguish themselves from their competitors and peers. In an era when it is important to keep the resume current and the contacts active, platform or presentation skills can provide a unique way of being recognized and appreciated.

5. Be open to new challenges and opportunities.

It makes no sense to embark on a new course with the expectation that it will meet all the anticipated needs with no new requirements from you. No matter how much you study the terrain, there will be unknown developments that occur and anticipated developments that do not occur. It is important to allow things to take place in their own time, and be willing to use your initiative and creativity in ways that you might not have anticipated. Even ideal jobs or ventures often require patience and proactive efforts in their early stages that we might not have expected. All too often people leave a developing situation too early. Sometimes the best opportunity erupts rather than flowing along predictably. Give your move a chance to succeed.

* * * * *

Career transitions can occur because you are dissatisfied with your job or career, want to approach retirement differently, have suffered a job loss, or have a simple desire to get more satisfaction from your work. You could be 17 or 70, looking for a new path to your passion or trying out a brand new arena in hopes of discovering your passion. Whatever the motivation to make a change, take into account that getting from where you are to where you want to be involves a transition. Learning what you can about yourself and what draws you to the field, as well as learning about the field itself are very important to your success. Both kinds of knowledge can be easily brushed aside on the assumption that neither requires any special consideration. When seeking greater satisfaction, long-term success, or a career highpoint, you give yourself a much better chance if you anticipate obstacles and opportunities by being knowledgeable of both. ◄

Answers and Actions Needed

1. Begin by looking at yourself and the circumstances surrounding your career transition. Be clear about where you want to go, what you want to do, and why.

2. **Get ready!** Read and talk to people knowledgeable of the field and those who know and support you. What do they say about your prospects for success? What advice do they give to assure your best chances for success?

3. Ask for help from your supporters, to assist you in evaluating things and making good choices.

4. **Use the help you get! Don't waste the time and efforts of others by ignoring legitimate feedback.** Accept it! Appreciate it! Evaluate it! And, use what you can!

5. **Have you made the commitment to take the new path seriously?** Prepare yourself to assure that the new effort reflects the best of you, your standards, and your values.

6. **Go for it!** Give the new venture the effort and time it takes to succeed. Don't give yourself a reason to look back with regret.

Consider these resources to add to your own:

- *Before You Quit Your Job* by Robert T. Kiyosaki and Sharon Lechter

- *Change Your Job, Change Your Life, Careering and Re-careering in the New Boom/Bust Economy* by Ron Krannich, Ph. D.

- *Do What You Are, Discover the Perfect Career* by Paul D. Tieger and Barbara Barron-Tieger

- *Live Your Dreams!* by Les Brown

- *Self* Magazine, **www.self.com**

- *The Consultant's Calling* by Geoffrey M. Bellman

- *Discover What You're Best At* by Linda Gale

- *Exploring Your Future, 200 Career Options* by Delmar Learning

- *Choosing Your Future* CD Series by Les Brown, **www.les-brown.com**

- *What Color Is Your Parachute? 2007: A Practical Manual for Job-Hunters and Career Changes* by Richard Nelson Bolles

- *The Over-40 Job Guide* by Kathryn and Ross Petras

CONCLUSION

WHEN you make the decision to reach beyond anyplace you have ever been, doors of opportunity begin to open. We all have potential beyond the fruits of our past and beyond what we can see. When we are ready, personally and professionally, and we go into action with methods that reflect our readiness, we draw people and other resources to us that can help us reach new heights. Doors open.

Whatever field you choose as a vehicle for bringing *your best stuff*, here's wishing you massive success. When you match your passion to achieve with the knowledge and resources to achieve, your chances for success are great. If your passion is matched with good people, good decision-making, and a workable plan, your chances for success are even greater. And if your passion is matched with a commitment to operate at the highest standard, based on the best information available, on the best advice available, and with the best resources available, your success will move to the next level, and the next, and the next. ➤